Multiple-Biometric Evaluation (MBE)
2010

Report on the Evaluation of 2D Still-Image Face Recognition Algorithms

NIST Interagency Report 7709

Patrick J. Grother, George W. Quinn and P. Jonathon Phillips

Image Group
Information Access Division
Information Technology Laboratory
National Institute of Standards and Technology

August 24, 2011

EXECUTIVE SUMMARY

Background

- Facial recognition algorithms from seven commercial providers, and three universities, were tested on one laboratory dataset and two operational face recognition datasets, one comprised of visa images, the other law enforcement mugshots. The population represented in these sets approaches 4 million, such that this report documents the largest public evaluation of face recognition technology to date. The project attracted participation from a majority of the known providers of FR technology including the largest commercial suppliers.

- Accuracy was measured for three applications: One-to-one verification (e.g. of e-passport holders); one-to-one verification against a claimed identity in an enrolled database (e.g. for driver's license re-issuance); and one-to-many search (e.g. for criminal identification or driver's license duplicate detection).

- Face images have been collected in law enforcement for more than a century, but their value for automated identification remains secondary to fingerprints. In a criminal investigation setting, face recognition has been used both in an automated mode and for forensic investigation. However, the limits of the technology have not previously been quantified publicly, and, in any case, are subject to improvement over time, and to the properties of the images in use.

- Core algorithmic capability is the major contributor to application-level recognition outcomes. A second critical factor is the quality of the input images; this is influenced by design of, and adherence to, image capture protocols (as codified by face recognition standards) and also by the behavior of the person being photographed (e.g. whether they face the camera). Some data collection protocols can embed a human adjudication of quality (e.g. of a visa image by a consular official) while others cannot maintain such tight quality controls (e.g. because of non-cooperative subjects in police booking processes).

- This is the first time NIST has reported accuracy of face *identification* algorithms. Prior tests have assumed an equivalence of a 1:N search as N 1:1 comparisons. This new protocol formally supports use of fast search algorithms such as indexing, partitioning and binning. The benefits are more accurate predictions of scalability to national-size populations.

- The project used archival imagery to assess core algorithmic capability of algorithms. It did not do an instrumented collection of images as might be used in a scenario or operational test. It therefore did not measure human-camera transactional performance parameters such as duration of use and outcome. These would be of vital interest in, for example, e-Passport gate applications.

Core Accuracy

- As with other biometrics, recognition accuracy depends strongly on the provider of the core technology. Broadly, there is an order of magnitude between the best and worst identification error rates.

- Biometric identification algorithms return candidate lists. These enumerate hypothesized identities for a search sample. Face identification algorithms can be set up to be used in two distinct modes. The first, *investigational* mode, assumes the existence of a corps of human face examiners retained to examine perhaps dozens of images on candidate lists. In the second, *identification* mode, the algorithm is set up with a high threshold to give very short candidate lists and a small chance that a non-matching candidate is returned. The most accurate investigational algorithms are not the most accurate identification algorithms.

- Using the most accurate face recognition algorithm, the chance of identifying the unknown subject (at rank 1) in a database of 1.6 million criminal records is about 92%. For other population sizes, this accuracy rate decreases linearly with the logarithm of the population size. In all cases a secondary (human) adjudication process will be necessary to verify that the top-rank hit is indeed that hypothesized by the system.

- When the most accurate algorithm is used in an investigational mode to provide trained examiners with the top fifty ranked candidates 97% of searches will yield the correct identity in a fixed population of 1.6 million subjects. In cases where the top 200 candidates are searched, the correct match is present 97.5% of the time. The hit rate increases roughly linearly with the log of the number of candidates inspected.

- In criminal law enforcement applications, where recidivism rates are high and a pool of examiners is available to traverse lengthy candidate lists, facial recognition algorithms offer high success rates. The more accurate

MBE-STILL REPORT	P = PITTPATT	R = SURREY U.	S = TSINGHUA U.	T = TOSHIBA	U = DALIAN TECH U.	PAGE 2 OF 61
PARTICIPANT KEY	V = NEC	W = L1 IDENTITY	X = COGNITEC	Y = SAGEM	Z = NEUROTECHNOLOGY	

algorithms reduce the workload on the examiner by placing mates at low (i.e. good) rank. We define an overall performance metric as the expected number of candidates an examiner will need to compare before the mate is found. If the most accurate algorithm is used for identification in the population of 1.6M, an examiner willing to review 50 candidates will only need to look at 3 on average before the mate is found.

— A facial recognition algorithm can also be used to do "lights-out" face identification. This requires application of a high decision threshold that implements a selectivity policy. Here a threshold is adopted that gives, on the average, a particular number of false candidates per search. For the most accurate face recognition algorithm tested here, if one in two searches produces a false candidate on average, the hit rate will be 89%. If workload demands on human adjudicators require that only one in ten searches produce a false candidate, the hit rate reduces to 85% and a different algorithm is best in this regime. These numbers apply to a population of 1.6M. The threshold will need to be estimated over a calibration process. This threshold will need to be increased as the enrolled population increases.

— Facial recognition algorithms are more accurate on the visa images than the mug shot images. The visa images were collected c. 1996-2001. The imaging processes used for their collection have improved since that time. The mug shot images are contemporary, and operationally representative of current law-enforcement collection practices. On these images, the face recognition accuracy results reported here will be closely predictive of those that would be encountered in any near term deployment.

— The visa images are collected with careful cooperation of the subject, active compliance by the photographer to the image collection specification, and a yes/no review by an official. The visa images are subject to losses associated with JPEG compression. The mugshot images, while less compressed and of generally higher resolution, exhibit considerable pose, illumination and expression variation. The most accurate algorithm demonstrates better tolerance of non-frontal pose than others.

— On the one database used in 2002, 2006 and 2010, the best verification accuracy measurement has declined by an order of magnitude in each four year period. On the visa images, false non-match rates (at a fixed false match rate of 0.001) have reduced from 0.2 in 2002, to 0.026 in 2006, and to 0.003 now. This result is achieved on a dataset that has various deviations from formal standards and best practices.

Exploitation of all historical encounters

— The test was executed using an Application Programming Interface (API) that supported identification of an image against all prior images of a subject, not just the most recent. This allowed the face recognition algorithm developers to exploit the historical record. It also assigned responsibility for fusion to the algorithm developers, who could implement early-stage template-level fusion or the simpler late stage score-level fusion.

— All recognition algorithms derive accuracy improvements when all past images are enrolled as a single template. The benefits are uniform across algorithms. The template size for a person enrolled with K images is, for all algorithms tested, closely K times the template size produced from a single image. These two facts suggest that common and simple techniques are sufficient to realize the available gain.

Speed and template size

— For the first time, this NIST evaluation measures and reports the speed of face recognition algorithms. The main result is atypical in biometrics: The most accurate algorithms are among the fastest. This departs from observations in fingerprint and iris trials that showed an industry-wide tradeoff between accuracy and computational expense.

— For search algorithms from the two most accurate providers, the time required to execute a one-to-many search against an enrolled population of 1.6 million people is 0.4 and 1.2 seconds respectively. This is the duration of the core search computation as measured on contemporary high-end yet standard hardware consisting of 16 computational cores, 192GB of main memory, and a 64 bit address space. It assumes that a search template has been prepared and transmitted to the matching engine.

— In most cases the time required to execute a search does not scale linearly with the size of the enrolled population. While the most accurate algorithm does scale linearly, the second most accurate algorithm scales such that a ten-fold increase in database size produces only a 1.3-fold increase in search duration. This behavior has been confirmed on sizes up to 1.6 million.

— Several participants elected to provide several implementations for evaluation. In so doing the provider demonstrated an ability to trade accuracy for speed, and to use large or small template sizes. This suggests a valuable ability to parameterize their algorithms to meet computational and accuracy requirements.

— The variance in search times is small. This arises because all search templates from a particular recognition algorithm have the same size. Across the algorithms tested here, template sizes range from about 5 to 75 kilobytes. By comparison, 90% of the law enforcement JPEG images used here are in the range 4 to 380 kilobytes, with median, 36 kilobytes.

Accuracy dependence on biographic data

— For the law enforcement images, it is empirically observed that men are more easily recognized than women, that heavier individuals are more easily recognized than lighter subjects, and that Asian subjects are more easily recognized than White. Younger persons are more difficult to recognize than their elders for some recognition algorithms, but the opposite is true for others.

— These results state marginal observations for the particular dataset. They do not explain the cause of the observation because there are confounding aspects to the data. So while men are more readily recognized than women, this may arise because women are generally shorter than men, and the height of a subject may induce non-optimal imaging angle if the camera height is not adjusted.

ABSTRACT

The paper evaluates state-of-the-art face identification and verification algorithms, by applying them to corpora of face images the population of which extends into the millions. Performance is stated in terms of core accuracy and speed metrics, and the dependence of these on population size and image properties are reported. One-to-many search algorithms are evaluated in terms of their use in both investigational and identification modes. Investigational performance has implications for workload on an examiner reviewing the results of a search. Identification performance, using a high score threshold, can support fully automated operation and decision making if some quantified level of false match is acceptable. In addition, the paper establishes an initial approach toward calibration of false match accuracy.

ACKNOWLEDGEMENTS

— The authors wish to thank Federal Bureau of Investigation for their support of this work.

— In addition, we appreciate Michael Garris' direction and tight coordination, and for his review of this document.

— In addition, NIST is indebted to Nick Orlans and the MITRE-led teams responsible for the intensive effort coordinating preparation of the public MEDS and private Photo-File image corpora.

— The authors thank Craig Watson, Brian Cochran and Wayne Salamon at NIST for their herculean and timely efforts to stand up the computers, power, air conditioning and software used to run the MBE-STILL trials.

— The authors thank Jay Scallan for review of the images.

— The authors are grateful to the experts who made comments on the drafts of the MBE-STILL Concept, Evaluation Plan and API document[1].

— Finally, the authors acknowledge the diligent work of the developers in implementing and supporting the MBE-protocol.

KEYWORDS

Face recognition; biometrics; verification; identification; recognition; identity management; watch-list; pattern recognition; reliability; scalability; calibration; mugshot.

DISCLAIMER

---

[1] See http://face.nist.gov/mbe/

TIMELINE OF THE MBE-STILL EVALUATION

Date	Activity
June 8, 2010	Release of the first draft of the public MBE-STILL report.
May 14, 2010	Window for submission of FR implementations to NIST closes
February 28, 2010	First FR implementations arrive at NIST
February 1, 2010	Release of the final Still Face Image Track - Concept, Evaluation Plan and API Version 1.0.0
January 27, 2010	Window for submission of FR implementations to NIST opens
December 15, 2009	Release of sample data: http://face.nist.gov/mbe/NIST_SD32v01_MEDS_I_face.zip
December 09, 2009	Second draft evaluation plan (revised version of this document) for public comment.
November 16, 2009	Initial draft evaluation plan circulated for public comment.
July 29, 2009	Project Initiation: Briefing to the FBI, *Face Recognition Testing Tailored to the FBI Application*, Patrick Grother, NIST.

October 2009	November 2009	December 2009	January 2010	February 2010

Su Mo Tu We Th Fr Sa
            1 2 3
4 5 6 7 8 9 10
11 12 13 14 15 16 17
18 19 20 21 22 23 24
25 26 27 28 29 30 31
	Su Mo Tu We Th Fr Sa
	1 2 3 4 5 6 7
	8 9 10 11 12 13 14
	15 16 17 18 19 20 21
	22 23 24 25 26 27 28
	29 30
		Su Mo Tu We Th Fr Sa
		       1 2 3 4 5
		6 7 8 9 10 11 12
		13 14 15 16 17 18 19
		20 21 22 23 24 25 26
		27 28 29 30 31
			Su Mo Tu We Th Fr Sa
			              1 2
			3 4 5 6 7 8 9
			10 11 12 13 14 15 16
			17 18 19 20 21 22 23
			24 25 26 27 28 29 30
			31
				Su Mo Tu We Th Fr Sa
				    1 2 3 4 5 6
				7 8 9 10 11 12 13
				14 15 16 17 18 19 20
				21 22 23 24 25 26 27
				28

March 2010	April 2010	May 2010	June 2010	July 2010

Su Mo Tu We Th Fr Sa
  1 2 3 4 5 6
7 8 9 10 11 12 13
14 15 16 17 18 19 20
21 22 23 24 25 26 27
28 29 30 31
	Su Mo Tu We Th Fr Sa
	           1 2 3
	4 5 6 7 8 9 10
	11 12 13 14 15 16 17
	18 19 20 21 22 23 24
	25 26 27 28 29 30
		Su Mo Tu We Th Fr Sa
		                1
		2 3 4 5 6 7 8
		9 10 11 12 13 14 15
		16 17 18 19 20 21 22
		23 24 25 26 27 28 29
		30 31
			Su Mo Tu We Th Fr Sa
			      1 2 3 4 5
			6 7 8 9 10 11 12
			13 14 15 16 17 18 19
			20 21 22 23 24 25 26
			27 28 29 30
				Su Mo Tu We Th Fr Sa
				             1 2 3
				4 5 6 7 8 9 10
				11 12 13 14 15 16 17
				18 19 20 21 22 23 24
				25 26 27 28 29 30 31

	Test and API Development	Test Execution	Analysis and Reporting	

VERSION HISTORY

Date	Activity
June 22, 2010	1/ Improved reporting of class B vs. class A results in INVESTIGATION 8. 2/ Added results for Y04 to pose/sex/age in Figure 20 and onwards. 3/ Replaced boxplots for FNMR by sex with tabulated values. 4/ Added verification results for R00, W10, W11 to Figure 12. 5/ Added tabulated values to graphs showing effect of population size, and effect of rank.
June 18, 2010	1/ Fixed incorrect identification of Dalian University of Technology 2/ Updated Figure 16 – LEO Selectivity by number of prior encounters to include more class C algorithms and all 1000 bootstrap estimates of selectivity. 3/ Added result for Y04 to verification results in Figures 12 and 15.
June 16, 2010	First publication of this document, NISTIR 7709
August 24, 2011	Added text to INVESTIGATION 11, p. 42, to indicate the roll of prior probabilities in interpreting high impostor scores.

TABLE OF CONTENTS

LIST OF FIGURES

LIST OF TABLES

TERMS AND DEFINITIONS

The abbreviations and acronyms of Table 1 are used in many parts of this document.

Table 1 – Abbreviations

FR	Face Recognition
MBE	NIST's Multiple Biometric Evaluation program
MBE-STILL	The track of the MBE concerned with recognition of 2D still images.
TPIR	True positive identification rate
FNIR	False negative identification rate
FPIR	False positive identification rate
FMR	False match rate
FNMR	False non-match rate
FTE	Failure to Enroll, also Failure to Enroll Rate.
Reliability	A Type I error rate expressing hit or miss rate.
Selectivity	A Type II error rate expressing false positive errors
DET	Detection error tradeoff characteristic: For verification this is a plot of FNMR vs. FMR (sometimes as normal deviates, sometimes on log-scales). For identification this is a plot of FNIR vs. FPIR.
ROC	Receiver Operating Characteristic
CMC	Cumulative Match Characteristics
SC 37	Subcommittee 37 of Joint Technical Committee 1 – developer of biometric standards
INCITS	InterNational Committee on Information Technology Standards
ISO/IEC 19794	ISO/IEC 19794-5: Information technology — Biometric data interchange formats — Part 5:Face image data. First edition: 2005-06-15. (See Bibliography entry).
I385	INCITS 385:2004 - U.S. precursor to the 19794-5 international standard
ANSI/NIST Type 10	The dominant container for facial images in the law enforcement world.
MEDS	Multiple Encounter Deceased Subjects
NIST	National Institute of Standards and Technology
PIV	Personal Identity Verification
SDK	The term Software Development Kit refers to any library software submitted to NIST. This is used synonymously with the terms "implementation" and "implementation under test".

1. MBE-STILL Goals and Objectives

Initiated in summer 2009, the Multi-biometric 2D Still-Face Recognition evaluation was undertaken with the following objectives.

— To respond to governmental and commercial requests to assess contemporary facial recognition (FR) implementations.

— To leverage massive operational corpora. The availability of images from large populations (in the millions) ensures statistical significance of all studies, particularly across demographic groups. The use of operational images brings greater operational relevance to the test results.

— To evaluate face recognition technologies in a proper one-to-many identification mode. This departs from many prior evaluations in which 1:N search accuracy was simulated via computation of N 1:1 comparisons[2].

— To report parameters important to implementers and procurers. These include template size and processing times.

1.1. MBE Context

The still-face recognition track is a standalone part of the larger MBE parent program. As depicted in Figure 1, MBE also includes tracks for recognition-from-video and face-iris portals. See http://face.nist.gov/mbe for the status of all MBE activities.

Figure 1 – Organization and documentation of the MBE

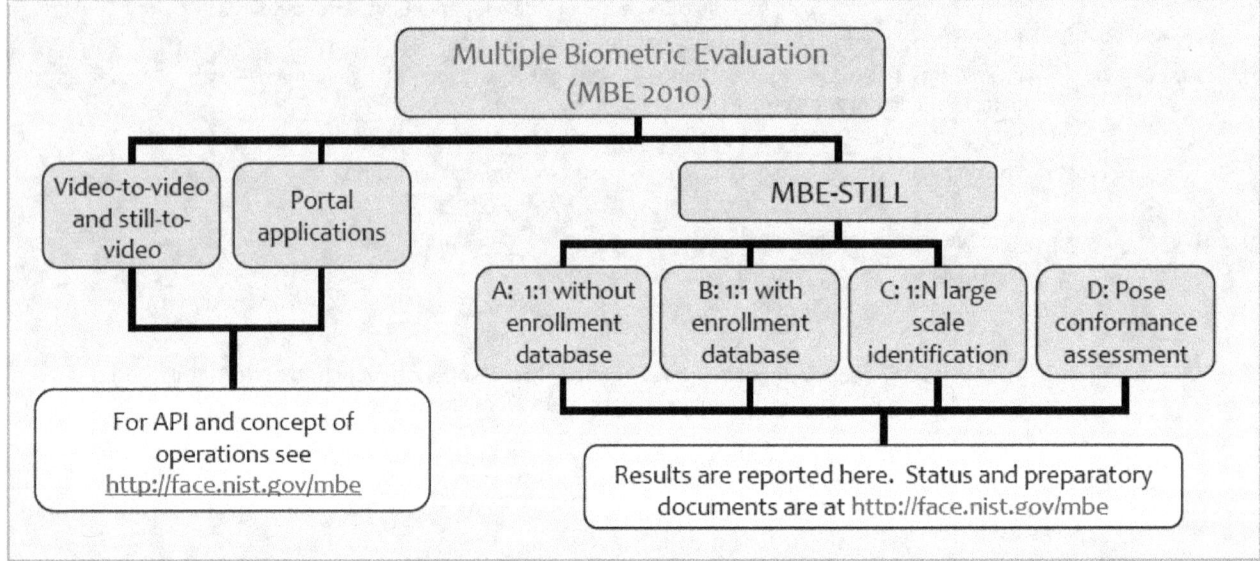

1.2. Market drivers

This test is intended to support a plural marketplace of face recognition systems. While the dominant application, in terms of revenue, has been one-to-many search for driving licenses and visa issuance, the deployment of one-to-one face recognition has re-emerged with the advent of the e-Passport verification projects[3]. In addition, there remains

---

[2] NIST has previously only modeled identification scenarios. The simplest simulation mimics a 1:N search by conducting N 1:1 comparisons.

[3] These match images acquired from a person crossing a border against the ISO/IEC 19794-5 facial image stored on the embedded ISO/IEC 7816 + ISO/IEC ISO 14443 chips. Such systems are fielded in Portugal (RAPID), Australia (SmartGate), Germany (EasyPASS) [NUPPENEY], the United Kingdom (UKBA) and elsewhere. Such systems can viably establish a low false acceptance policy because traditional immigration processes are available to those rejected. Accuracy is dependent on both the quality of the standardized e-Passport image, and on the images produced by the automated access-control gate. The gate design typically includes supplemental lighting, and some mechanism to adjust for the height of the traveler.

considerable activity in the use of face recognition in a number of identification applications. The list given in Table 2 differentiates applications by population size and the kinds of images used.

Table 2 – Biometric identification applications

#	Application	Open set	Coop	Typical population size	Kind of reference or enrolled image	Search image
1	De-duplication e.g. for benefits fraud detection	Y	C	Starting at zero, increasing to millions, as database grows	Often collected for a credential, e.g. a visa or driver's license. Ideally ISO/IEC 19794-5 compliant.	Same as reference
2	Web-search. Social networking consolidation.	Y	N	Millions	Zero or more images existing on various web pages. Usually uncontrolled.	Also uncontrolled.
3	Forward criminal search	Y	CNU	Millions	Mugshot collected incident to an arrest (i.e. more or less compliant to ANSI/NIST Type 10 mugshot standards)	Usually the same properties as the reference
4	Reverse criminal search; unsolved photo file as defined in [EBTS].	Y	CNU	Tens of thousands	The photograph of a person associated with an adverse event.	Mugshot.
5	Watch-list, covert surveillance.	Y	N	Tens of thousands	Varied. Sometimes controlled but often adverse.	Varied, often dissimilar to the reference
6	Access-control without presentation of a credential or PIN	Y	C	Thousands	Attended enrollment in good conditions. Ideally ISO/IEC 19794-5 compliant.	Similar to reference, but with relaxed imaging constraints
7	Cruise-ship	N	C	Thousands	Controlled photo collected at time of boarding.	
8	Disaster post-mortem	N Y	N	Hundreds, thousands	Varied.	Varied.
9	Column 4 gives cooperation of the subjects: C = cooperative, N = non-cooperative, U= actively uncooperative or evasive.					

1.3.   Application scenarios

The MBE-STILL activity includes one-to-one verification and one-to-many identification tests, as described in Table 3. Class A might be preferred by academic institutions because the API supports the elemental hypothesis testing verification function: "Are the images from the same person or not?"

Table 3 – Subtests supported under the MBE still-face activity

	Class A	Class B	Class C	Class D
Application area	1:1 verification without an enrollment database	1:1 verification with an enrollment database	1:N identification	Pose calibration
Description	Verification scenarios in which still images are compared.	Verification scenarios in which images are compared with entries in an enrolled database.	Close-to-operational use of face recognition technologies in identification applications in which the enrolled dataset could contain images from up to three million persons.	Assess whether the orientation of the head meets frontal imaging pose specifications.
Required	Yes, all participants must submit algorithms.	Optional	Optional	Optional
Participation	10	7	8	3

1.4.   Offline testing

While this set of tests is intended as much as possible to mimic operational reality, this remains an offline test executed on databases of images. The intent is to assess the core algorithmic capability of face recognition algorithms. This test was conducted purely offline. That is, it did not include a live human-presents-to-camera component. Offline testing is attractive because it allows uniform, fair, repeatable, and efficient evaluation of the underlying technologies. Testing of implementations under a fixed API allows for a detailed set of performance related parameters to be measured.

2.   Participation

The MBE program was open to participation worldwide. There were no requirements for entry, other than an ability to implement the interface protocol specifications. In the case of MBE-STILL, this requires conformance to a "C" language API which in turn requires software engineering skills associated with technology developers and researchers. As with all NIST technology evaluations, NIST did not charge a fee to participate.

This report documents SDK-based implementations submitted during a window of participation which ran from January 27, 2010 through May 14, 2010. The participants are tabulated in Table 4.

Table 4 – MBE-STILL Face Recognition Technology Providers

#	Organization	Code	Class A: One-to-one verification	Class B: One-to-one verification with enrollment db	Class C: One-to-many identification	Class D: Pose conformance
1.	Cognitec	X	Yes	Yes	Yes	
2.	Dalian University of Technology	U	Yes			
3.	L1 Identity Solutions	W	Yes	Yes	Yes	
4.	NEC	V	Yes	Yes	Yes	
5.	Neurotechnology	Z	Yes	Yes	Yes	
6.	Pittsburg Pattern Recognition	P	Yes	Yes	Yes	Yes
7.	Sagem	Y	Yes		Yes	Yes
8.	Surrey University	R	Yes			
9.	Toshiba	T	Yes	Yes	Yes	
10.	Tsinghua University	S	Yes	Yes	Yes	Yes

3.   Datasets

This report documents the use of four datasets.

— **LEO:** The primary dataset consists of facial images collected by various law enforcement (LEO) agencies and transmitted to the FBI as part of various criminal records checks. This is known as the FBI Photo File.

— **DOS / Natural:** The secondary dataset consists of non-immigrant visa images. It is used here for one-to-many identification purposes.

— **DOS / HCINT:** This extract of DOS / Natural was used in the FRVT 2002 evaluation [FRVT2002], and subsequently the FRVT 2006 follow-on [FRVT 2006].

— **SANDIA:** A set of high resolution frontal-face images used as the high resolution dataset in the FRVT 2006 evaluation [FRVT2006]. The Sandia dataset was collected at the Sandia National Laboratory. Enrollment face images were collected with controlled illumination with cooperation from the subjects. Verification images were collected in two modes: First, with controlled illumination, and second without it. The Sandia images were taken with a 4 Megapixel Canon PowerShot G2.

The properties are summarized in Table 5.

Table 5 – Image dataset descriptions

Property	LEO	DOS / Natural	DOS / HCINT	Sandia
Collection, environment	Law enforcement booking	Visa application process	Visa application process	Dedicated laboratory collection.
Collection era	~ 1960s-2008	~ 1996-2002	~ 1996-2002	
Live scan, Paper	Live, few paper	Mostly live	Mostly live	Live
Documentation	See NIST Special Database 32 Volume 1, available 12/09[4].		See NIST IR 6965 [FRVT2002]	See NISR IR 7408 [FRVT 2006]
Image size	Various, 480x640, 240x240, 768x960	Most 300 x 252	Most 300 x 252	
Compression	JPEG ~ 20:1	JPEG	JPEG mean size 9467 bytes. See [FRVT2002b]	JPEG, very little compression
Eye to eye distance	mean=156, sd=46	Median = 71 pixels	Median = 71 pixels	Controlled, mean = 350 Uncontrolled, mean = 110
Frontal	Moderate control. Known profile images excluded.	Yes, well controlled	Yes, well controlled	Controlled: yes Uncontrolled: yes
Full frontal geometry	Mostly not. Varying amounts of the torso are visible.	Yes, in most cases. Faces are more cropped (i.e. smaller background) than ISO FF requires.	Yes, in most cases. Faces are more cropped (i.e. smaller background) than ISO FF requires.	
Use in MBE-STILL	1:1 and 1:N	1:N	1:1	1:1
Parent	Operational data	Operational data	This is an extract of DOS / Natural persons 18+ years with 3 or more images. Introduces selection bias toward young men.	Self

3.1. Sizes of datasets

The databases are characterized by population sizes well in excess of all published biometric tests. The numbers of subjects and images are given in Table 6.

Table 6 – Image dataset sizes

#	Quantity	LEO	DOS / Natural	DOS / HCINT	Sandia
1.	Number of subjects	1802874	5738141	37440	263
2.	Num. subjects with 1 images	1428308	5294708	0	0
3.	Num. subjects with 2 images	253564	388975	0	0
4.	Num. subjects with 3 images	69527	44539	30701	2
5.	Num. subjects with 4 images	26509	7554	5069	12
6.	Num. subjects with 5 images	11659	1647	1111	14
7.	Num. subjects with 6 images	5825	477	376	1
8.	Num. subjects with 7 or more	7482 (Person max 26)	201 (Person max 13)	193 (Person max 13)	234
9.	Num. images in total	2407768	6249392	121589	13854
10.	Num. subjects used	1800000, selected randomly from line 1.	1850000	36000 in 12 partitions of 3000 subjects.	263
11.	Num. subjects used only as impostor / non-mates	200000, selected randomly from line 10.	50000	3000 from partition k+1 mod 12	0

---

[4] NIST Special Database 32, Volume 1, is available at: http://face.nist.gov/mbe/NIST_SD32v01_MEDS_I_face.zip. This link is temporary. The database will ultimately be linked from http://face.nist.gov/mbe.

12.	Num. images used only as impostor / non-mates	200000, last image of subjects selected randomly	50000	6000, two images used separately	0
13.	Num. subjects used in enrollment processes	1600000, selected randomly from line 10.	1800000	3000 per partition	263
14.	Num. images used in enrollment processes	1816170	1816743	3000 per partition	3404
15.	Num. images excluded	Profile, corrupt JPEG,	0	9, corrupt similarity files in FRVT 2002.	

3.2. Public sample images

NIST released the MEDS dataset in January 2010. MEDS stands for Multiple Encounter Deceased Subjects. The MEDS dataset is a representative and public sample of the non-public LEO set used in MBE-STILL. Specific examples are shown in Figure 2, Figure 3 and Figure 4 with respective commentaries.

Figure 2 – Examples of law enforcement images (I)

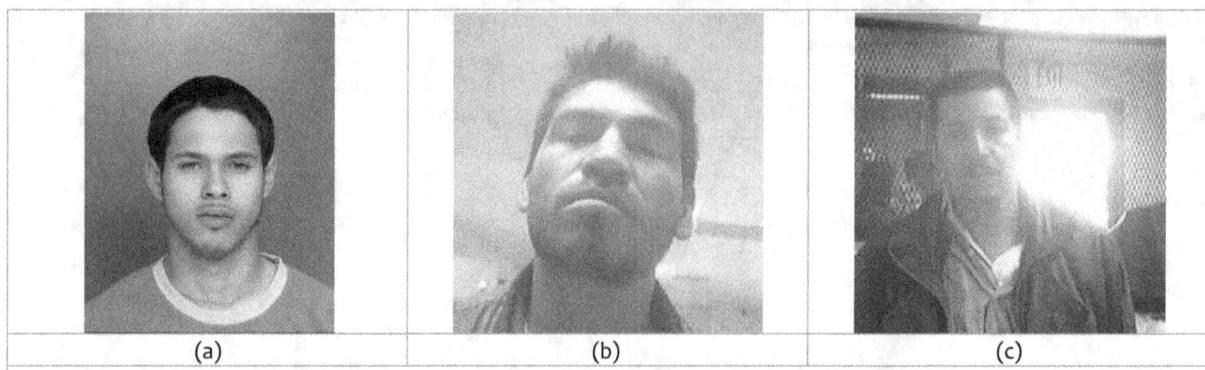

| (a) | (b) | (c) |

Image (a) is about as conformant to facial recognition image standards as the law enforcement images get. The remaining images shown here are grossly non-conformant. Image (b) has a pitch angle that is likely fatal to automated facial recognition algorithms, lens distortion associated with the camera being too close to the subject, poor uniformity of illumination and low contrast. Image (b) and (c) have image dimensions 240x240 indicative of capture using a webcam. Such images can originate in non-traditional law-enforcement sites, such as at a border crossing.

Figure 3 – Examples of law enforcement images (II)

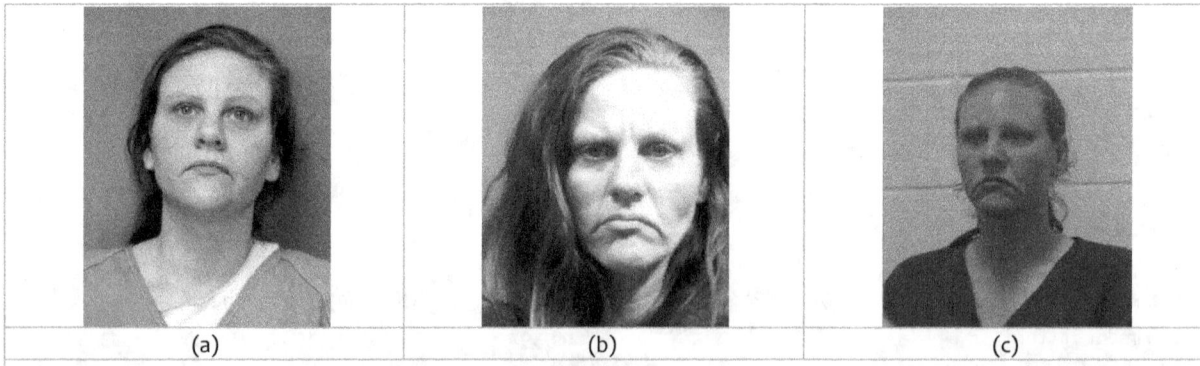

| (a) | (b) | (c) |

Three images of one person from the MEDS dataset. All three images are of size 480x600 pixels. All depart from defined standards: In image (a) the subject's pitch angle is slightly too high; in image (c) the yaw angle is well beyond the 5 degrees limit established in standards; in image (b) there is considerable saturation and non-uniformity of the lighting

Figure 4 - Examples of law enforcement images (III)

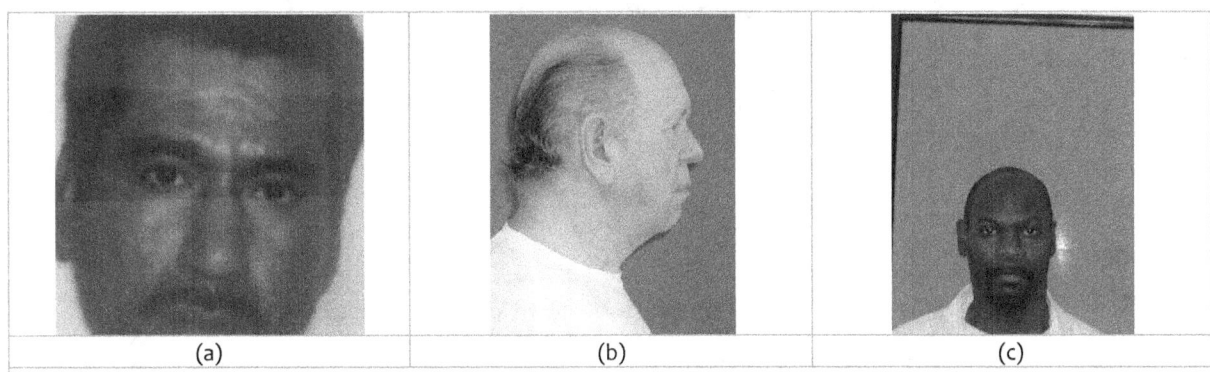

(a)	(b)	(c)

Examples of non-conformant images. Image (a) is a photograph of a photograph. Image (b) is a profile - these have been collected for at least a century by law-enforcement agencies. Commercial products cannot match these with other profiles, nor frontals. They are often present in the dataset but mislabeled (in standard record header) as being frontal images. Such images often produce failures to enroll (FTE) because face and eye-detection algorithms fail. In MBE-STILL, most profile images were dropped from the study; some images remain and these decrease hit rates. Image (c) has size 768x960 pixels. It is likely to be recognized because face detectors in MBE-STILL expected wide variation in image placement.

4. Metrics

4.1. Verification

The fundamental matching error rates are defined in Table 7 and Table 8.

Table 7 -- Definition of False Non-match Rate

FNMR(T)	=	$\dfrac{\text{Number of genuine comparisons with similarity score less than threshold, T.}}{\text{Number of genuine comparisons attempted}}$	Equation 1

Table 8 -- Definition of False Match Rate

FMR (T)	=	$\dfrac{\text{Number of impostor comparisons that produce a score greater than or equal to threshold, T.}}{\text{Number of impostor comparisons attempted}}$	Equation 2

These are plotted as a DET characteristic.

Table 9 – Verification Performance characteristics

Metric	Measured over	Definition
DET	Searches with and without mates	The receiver operating characteristic is a plot of FNMR(T) vs. FMR(T), where T is any real-valued threshold.

4.2. Identification

MBE-STILL tested only open-set identification algorithms. This means that some searches have no enrolled mate. This is operationally typical: some subjects have not been issued a visa or drivers license before; some law enforcement searches are from first-time offenders. Searches for these people should return zero identities.

Open-set applications require estimation of two error rates: Type I errors are those in which a person's biometric is incorrectly not associated with its enrolled mate; Type II errors are those in which a person's biometric data is

associated with other enrollees' data. Table 14 defines metrics for Type I identification errors used in this report, and notes various synonyms and complementary terms.

Table 15 defines metrics for Type II errors.

In a closed-set application, all searches have an enrolled mate. Operationally closed-universe applications are rare. One example is a cruise ship in which all passengers are enrolled and all searches should produce one, and only one, identity. Another example is forensic identification of dental records from an aircraft crash. Most practical applications of biometric identification are open-set problems. MBE-STILL did not address closed-set applications. This means that the SDK under test could make no assumption about whether or not it should return a high-scoring result.

Table 10 – Definition of True Positive Identification Rate

TPIR (R,T,L)	=	Num. searches with enrolled mate reported as candidate with score ≥ threshold, T, and rank ≤ R on a candidate list of length L <hr>Num. searches with enrolled mate	Equation 3

Table 11 – Definition of False Positive Identification Rate

FPIR (T,L)	=	Num. searches without enrolled mate yielding one or more candidates with score ≥ threshold, T when candidate list is of length L <hr>Num. searches without enrolled mate	Equation 4

Table 12 – Definition of Reliability

REL (T,L)	=	TPIR(N,T, L) where N is the size of the enrolled population	Equation 5

Table 13 – Definition of Selectivity

SEL (T,L)	=	Num. candidates with score ≥ threshold, T produced in searches without enrolled mate, when candidate list is of length L <hr>Num. searches without enrolled mate	Equation 6

Table 14 – Definitions of Type I error rates

Metric	Measured over	Definition	Related terms
True Positive Identification Rate (TPIR)	Searches for which a mate is present in the enrolled dataset.	Table 10. Fraction of identification searches for which the enrolled mate is present on the candidate list with rank less than or equal to R, and score greater than or equal to threshold, T. **Special cases:** 1. The rank requirement can be set to be difficult, i.e. R = 1, or absent (i.e. R = N, where N is the number of enrolled identities) or any value in between. 2. The threshold requirement can be difficult (i.e. high value of T), or absent (i.e. T = 0), or any value in between.	Hit Rate and Reliability of synonyms FNIR and miss rate are synonyms for the complement 1 – FNIR
FNIR	See TPIR	FNIR = 1 – TPIR(R, T,L)	FNIR
Miss Rate	See TPIR	FNIR(R, T,L)	FNIR
Hit Rate	See TPIR	TPIR(R, T,L)	FNIR

Table 15 – Definitions of Type II error rates

Metric	Measured over	Definition	Related terms
False Positive Identification Rate (FPIR)	Searches for which a mate is not present in the enrolled dataset.	Table 11. Fraction of identification searches for which any (i.e. one or more) enrolled identities on a candidate list of length L are returned with score greater than or equal to threshold T.	Selectivity
Selectivity	See FPIR	Table 13. The mean, over a set of searches, of the number of candidates returned for which the score is greater than or equal to a threshold, T.	False positive identification rate

From these metrics the primary performance characteristics are defined in Table 16.

Table 16 – Identification Performance characteristics

Metric	Measured over	Definition
CMC	Searches with mates	The cumulative match characteristic is a plot of $1 - FNIR(R, 0, L)$ vs. R, with $1 \leq R \leq L$
ROC	Searches with and without mates	The receiver operating characteristic is a plot of $REL(T,L)$ vs. $SEL(T,L)$

4.2.1. Best practice testing requires execution of searches with and without mates

MBE-STILL embedded 1:N searches of two kinds: Those for which there is an enrolled mate, and those for which there is not. However, it is common to conduct only mated searches. This is bad practice because if the information that a mate always exists is revealed to a test participant, or can be reasonably assumed, then unrealistic gaming of the test is possible.

The cumulative match characteristic is computed from candidate lists produced in mated searches. Even if the CMC is the only metric of interest, the actual trials executed in a test should nevertheless include searches for which no mate exists. MBE-STILL reserved disjoint populations of subjects for executing true non-mate searches.

4.2.2. Rank and threshold censoring

In a real operation, a search against an enrolled population of size N could produce a candidate list with N entries. This would occur if the operating threshold was set to zero. Practically, systems use an internal threshold T and they may only report a finite number of candidates, e.g. only the top 60.

4.2.3. Bootstrap uncertainty estimation

Bootstrapping is an empirical method of measuring the variability of a statistic, often employed when the variability cannot be determined analytically. In the context of this evaluation, bootstrapping is sometimes used to measure the distribution of error statistics (i.e. FNMR or FMR) at a fixed threshold. Each bootstrap iteration samples with replacement from the original set of comparisons. The statistic of interest is then computed over the sampled data. This process is repeated for a large number of bootstrap iterations to produce a distribution of the measured statistic. Bootstrapping relies on several assumptions, including the assumption that the sample data is *iid* (independent and identically distributed). However, when different comparisons involve the same individual, the comparisons are likely to be correlated due to the existence of Doddington's zoo [DODDINGTON]. Thus, the independence assumption is violated. Determining the effect this has on the bootstrapped distributions is beyond the scope of this evaluation, but the likely result is an underestimation of the variability of FNMR and/or FMR in some cases.

4.3. Failure to acquire

Some biometric algorithms may fail to convert some input samples to templates. This can be the result of a software bug (e.g. buffer overrun), or an algorithmic limitation (e.g. failure to find eyes in small images), or an elective refusal to process the input (e.g. because the image is assessed to have insufficient quality). For these events, the result is a template of zero size. The NIST API specification required the verification function to nevertheless process such templates. For identification the result of a failed template generation was not passed to the search function.

NOTE: Some face recognition algorithms would fail to produce a template when the result of decoding a broken JPEG image was provided to the implementation under test. This is not really the fault of the implementation. MBE-STILL removed all broken images before the test. The term "broken" in this context means a malformed JPEG file, e.g. one that is syntactically incorrect, up to and including truncation of the JPEG stream. Integrators will generally need to detect broken data before passing to the SDK[5].

5. Properties of the implementations

The objectives of the test were to

— Assess core capability of face recognition technology.

— Be fair tests

— Be repeatable

— Not constrain or favor particular algorithms.

Accordingly the test was administered with the following aspects.

Table 17 -- Test design considerations

Black Box Testing	NIST specified a "C" API and required MBE STILL participants to hide their face recognition algorithms behind it. The resulting technologies were submitted to NIST as windows or linux libraries. This constitutes black-box testing, i.e. the test laboratory has no exposure to, nor interest in, how the technology works.
Fair repeatable testing	The software implementations were given face images stored on hard drives. This defines offline testing (versus online testing where a person appears before a camera). Offline testing allows use of very large datasets (giving statistical significance), supports fair comparative testing, and allows experiments to be exactly repeated.
Modular components	The main operations supported are template generation (conversion of facial imagery to a proprietary, trade-secret, mathematical representation), template comparison for one-to-one verification, and template search for one-to-many identification.
Support for vendor-defined sample fusion	One or more face images of a person are bundled together and passed to template generation routines as a single object. This allows the implementation to fuse information derived from any or all of those images.
Separated verification and identification tests	The outputs of verification runs are real-valued similarity scores. These primarily support computation of the Receiver Operating Characteristic (ROC) as the basic statements of biometric accuracy.
	The outputs of identification runs are candidate lists which embed hypothesized identities for the search image. Each hypothesized identity is accompanied by a real valued similarity score. Candidate lists are sorted in decreasing order of that score. Candidate lists are of length 200, unless stated otherwise. Identification systems rarely return a score for all enrolled identities.
Support multistage matching identification algorithms	For reasons of efficiency, biometric identification systems can embed a multi-stage matching process that uses successively more accurate but more computationally expensive algorithms to reduce the population of candidate identities from an initial large value.
	MBE-STILL is a black box test in which templates embed vendor-defined mathematical representation of the face that are trade secrets. The API regards a template as a blob of binary data. Internally a provider may embed several different facial representations that can be used conditionally during a search. Thus a template of measureable size T could be composed of say two parts. A small template of size T_1 for efficient search, and another for expensive end-stage matching. This might have size T_2 such that $T = T_1 + T_2$ and $T_2 > T_1$.
Asymmetric Templates	Templates were generated for the specific purpose of enrollment, verification or identification. That is the templates have assigned roles. Templates are not used in other roles. This allows enrollment

---

[5] For all images, NIST tested JPEG conformance by ignoring any file for which "djpeg -fast -outfile /dev/null image.jpg" gave any output to stdout or stderr (djpeg is the command-line JPEG decompressor supplied in the IJG JPEG implementation www.ijg.org).

templates to have a different size than an identification template, for example.

Experimental method: The face recognition implementations submitted to MBE-STILL were tested in a black box manner. The mathematical representation of facial input data was stored as a proprietary template. The content of a template is unknown and non-standard. It is always a trade secret. The SDK was used as follows.

— The SDK under test was initialized. For one-to-many enrollments, the SDK was informed of the size of the population.

— The NIST test harness bundled k ≥1 images of a person were bundled into a MULTIFACE data structure.

— The MULTIFACE was passed to the template generation function of the SDK under test.

— The template was stored.

— In addition templates were concatenated to form an enrollment database (EDB).

— For one-to-one comparisons two isolated templates were passed to the SDK's comparison engine.

— For one-to-many searches, the SDK was initialized. The SDK would typically read the EDB into main memory.

— For one-to-many searches, a template was passed to the search function and it returned a candidate list.

— For one-to-one searches with an enrolment database, the template would be passed to the search function with an explicit claim to a particular identity. The SDK returns a comparison score.

NIST stored comparison scores and candidate lists and later used these in computation of the metrics of section 0.

6. Results

The results are presented as series of "investigations". Each addresses one quantitative aspect of performance.

INVESTIGATION 1. *Investigation-mode one-to-many search accuracy*
Are there accuracy differences between suppliers?

Demand driver: There are many applications of biometric identification algorithms. As summarized in Table 2, applications are differentiated by population sizes and the kinds of images being compared. However, in most applications, the core accuracy of a facial recognition algorithm is the most important performance variable. It quantifies the ability to answer the question are two samples from the same person, or not.

Experimental method: NIST used participants' class C SDKs to enroll images from each of N subjects to form an enrollment database containing N templates. A template is an entirely vendor-defined and non-standard blob of data. It is not suitable for interoperable interchange between systems. The template contains at least one mathematical representation of the face of the person in the input image.

Two sets were used:

- LEO: The values of N were 10 thousand, 80 thousand, 320 thousand and 1.6 million. The enrollment sets are simple random samples from the parent set of 1.6M persons. The sets are otherwise not subsets of each other. Mated and non-mated searches were run against these enrollments. The number of mated searches was M = 9240, 40000, 40000 and 40000 respectively for the four enrolled population sizes.

  In all cases, subjects were enrolled with $k \geq 1$ images. These were the oldest to the second-to-most recent image of a subject. Searches were made using $k = 1$ images per person. This was the most recent image of the subject.

- DOS / Natural: The values of enrolled population size N were 83981, 388800 and 1800000. In all cases, subjects were enrolled with $k \geq 1$ images. These were the oldest to the second-to-most recent image of a subject.

In each search, the SDK under test was asked to report the top 200 candidates.

Results: The candidate lists from mated searches in the LEO dataset were used to compute the cumulative match characteristic of Figure 5. The population size was 1.6M. The table to the right of the figure shows the rank 1 hit rate. There is more than a factor of five range in the observed miss rates (i.e. 1-TPIR), from 0.08 to 0.42. In addition, some identification algorithms produce more rapidly rising CMCs. This is a valuable property with implications for the workload on an examiner tasked with finding a mate on a candidate list. This aspect is quantified later in this report.

Conclusions: As with other biometrics, accuracy of facial recognition implementations varies greatly across the industry. Absent other performance or economic parameters, users should prefer the most accurate algorithm. Note, however, that the results of this section are entirely rank-based – the CMC computations ignore score information. This befits use of face recognition in the investigational mode in which an examiner is willing to traverse candidate lists looking for mates. Subsequent investigations in this report consider threshold-based metrics appropriate for identification mode applications. There, the leading algorithms are different from those listed above.

Note that the absolute values of identification accuracy will always depend on the dataset used, specifically to the properties of the images in use. In particular this study includes some residual non-frontal images that eluded detection during the data preparation phase. These images include some 90-degree profiles, and, somewhat more frequently, images in which the face is at a 45 or 60 degree yaw angle to the camera. These images usually cause complete recognition failure and depress overall error rates

Figure 5 – Identification accuracy vs. candidate rank

LEO (N = 1600000)

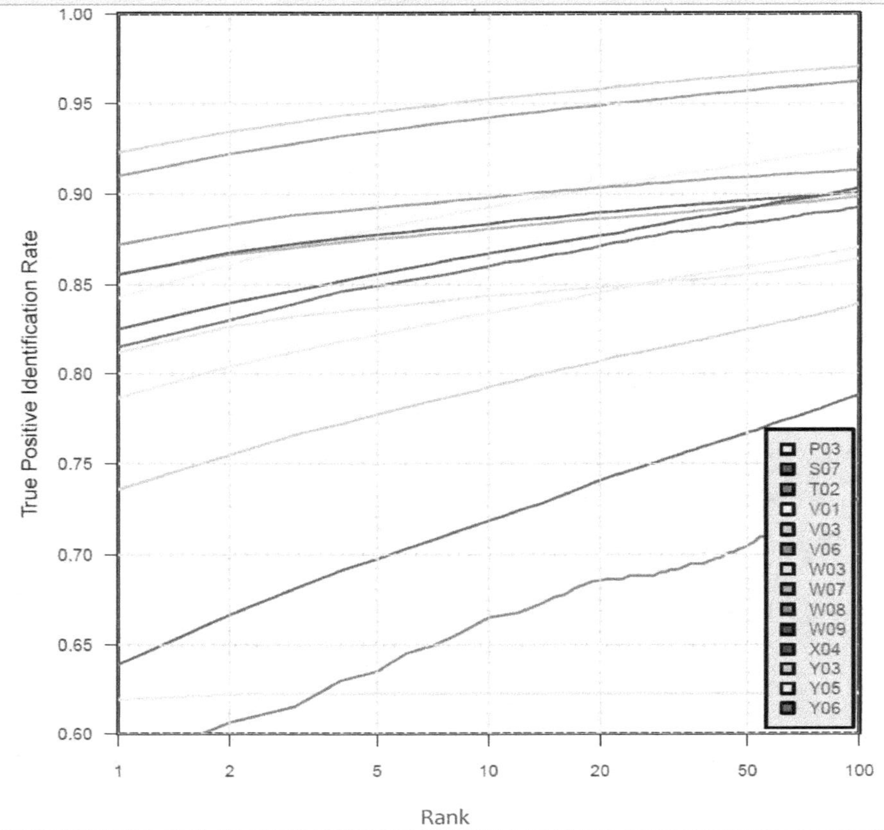

DOS / Natural (N=1800000)

Number of searches with mate = 40000

Number of searches without mate = 40000

The vertical axis plots Equation 3, CMC(R) = TPIR(R, T, L) with T=0 and L = 200.

The next rows give CMC(1) = TPIR(1,0,200)

SDK	V03	V06	W08	W07	W09	V01	X04	Y06	W03	Y05	Y03	S07	P03	T02
CMC(1)	0.92	0.91	0.87	0.86	0.86	0.84	0.83	0.82	0.81	0.79	0.74	0.64	0.62	0.58

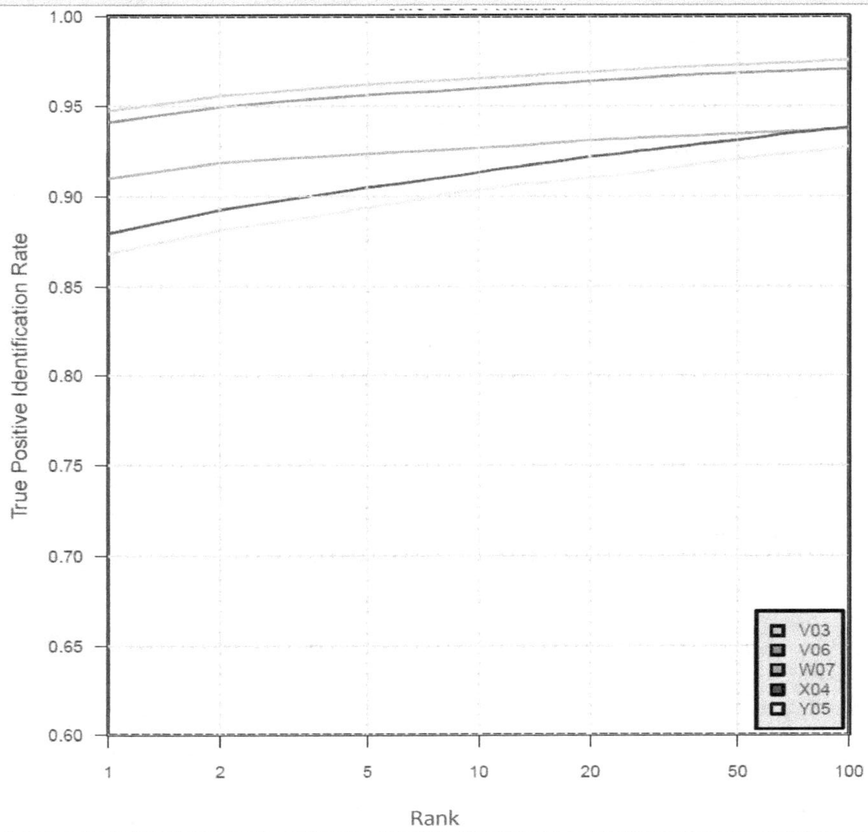

Number of searches with mate = 40000

Number of searches without mate = 40000

The vertical axis plots Equation 3, CMC(R) = TPIR(R, T, L) with T=0 and L = 200.

The next rows give CMC(1) = TPIR(1,0,200)

SDK	V03	V06	W07	X04	Y05
CMC(1)	0.95	0.94	0.91	0.88	0.87

Demand driver: Fingerprint identification systems are most commonly used without exhaustive review of a candidate list[6]. Face-based systems can also be used in this identification mode. While higher error rates are typically higher, these may be useful and tolerable given the longstanding acceptance of face images in government issued credentials such as passports and driving licenses. In the one-to-many mode, duplicate enrollments are detected if and only if the comparison score is at or above some threshold.

Prior work: A number of un-published tests have been conducted, usually as part of procurement processes. Prior NIST tests of facial recognition technology have computed identification accuracy from a complete set of N one-to-one comparison scores.

Experimental method: This investigation uses identically the same candidate lists produced in the prior investigations. Here the score values produced are not ignored; they are used to compute threshold-based estimates of accuracy. The result is plotted as a Receiver Operating Characteristic (ROC) which plots reliability against selectivity as a parametric function of threshold, i.e. REL(T) vs. SEL(T). Rank is completely ignored. While any set of real-valued thresholds can be used, we adopted the set of all observed genuine scores.

Results:

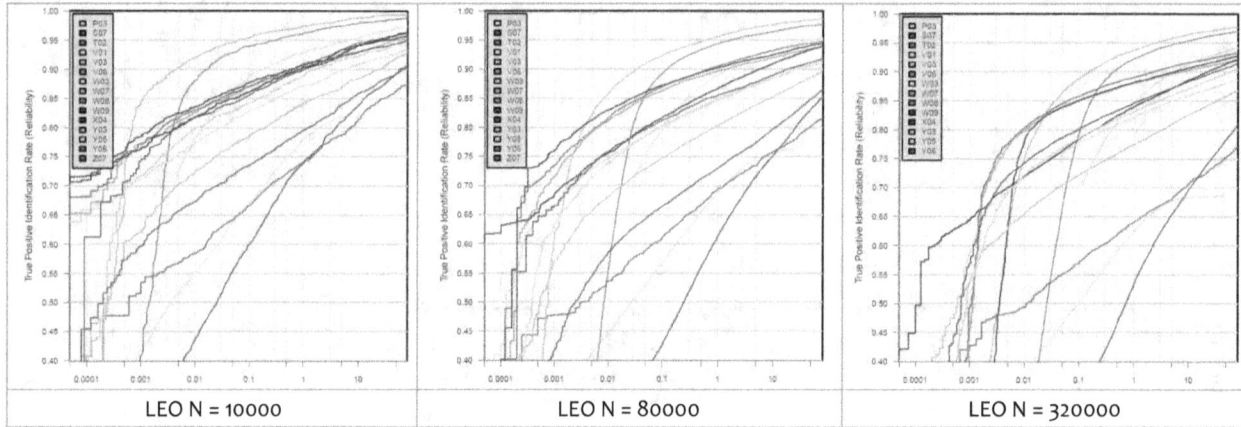

| LEO N = 10000 | LEO N = 80000 | LEO N = 320000 |

---

[6] This does not apply to latent fingerprint systems where examiners are involved in variety of ways [MEAGHER], including the forensic markup before a search, and in the adjudication of results from a search.

Figure 6 shows the ROC for the SDKs operating on a population of 1.6M. The three subfigures show the ROCs for populations of 10K, 80K and 320K. The four ROCs are essentially horizontal translations of each other because the occurrence of high scoring non-matches is approximately linear in the population size.

This ROC is one of the more interesting ROCs plots published in biometric test reports, because the ROCs cross. We can identify three selectivity regimes as follows. When selectivity is high (when SEL > 1, for example), the best performing *investigation* mode SDK, V03, gives the highest reliability. This is consistent with the cumulative match characteristics plotted earlier. However, in the middle-selectivity regime (SEL < 0.1), the reliability of V03 drops off rapidly such that the W08 SDK initially gives the best reliability. This lasts until the low selectivity region, SEL < 0.005, where ultimately X04 is most reliable. In this *identification* mode, the X04 SDK will produce false matches for only one in every 10000 searches, but reliability has dropped so that more than one in two mated searches will give a miss. Note that at such low selectivities, when the operating threshold T is high, the best *investigational* SDKs fail essentially completely (i.e. reliability approaches zero).

Conclusions: The leading algorithms at high selectivity rates are not the leading algorithms at low selectivity rates. However the declared intent of MBE-STILL was to support recognition in an *investigation* mode. Without soliciting SDKs for the specific purpose of identification mode operation, the results given in

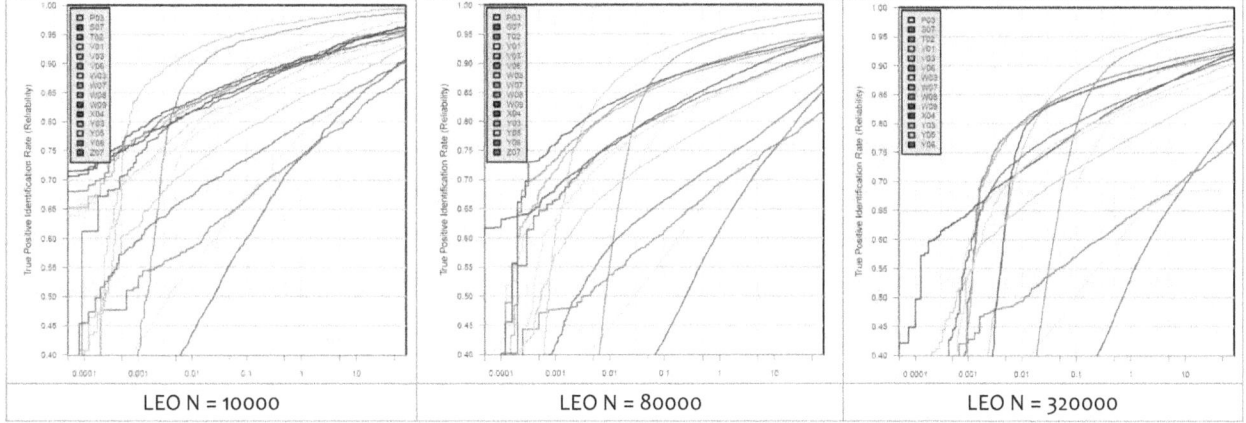

Figure 6 may not reveal the full potential for lights out identification with LEO images

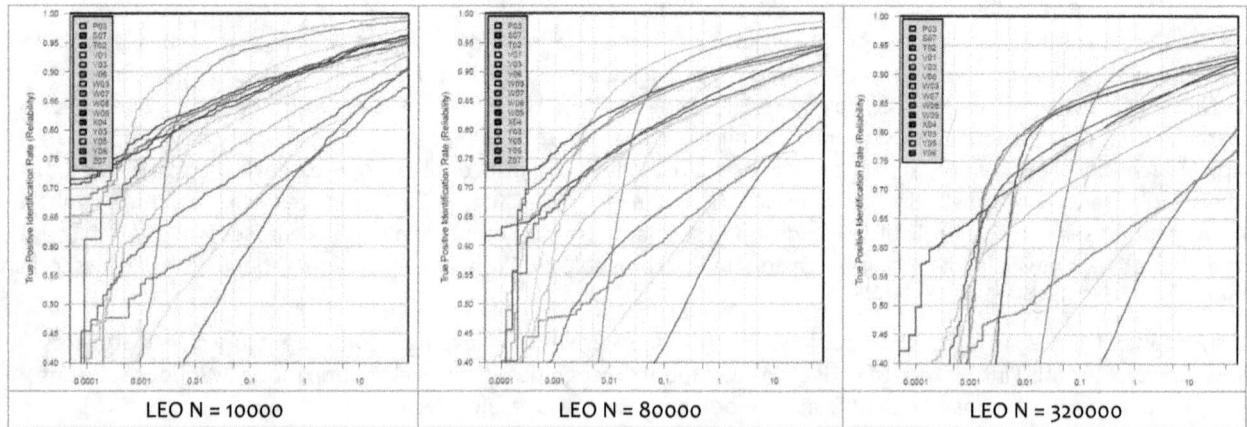

| LEO N = 10000 | LEO N = 80000 | LEO N = 320000 |

Figure 6 – Identification rate vs. selectivity

(a)

LEO (N = 1600000)

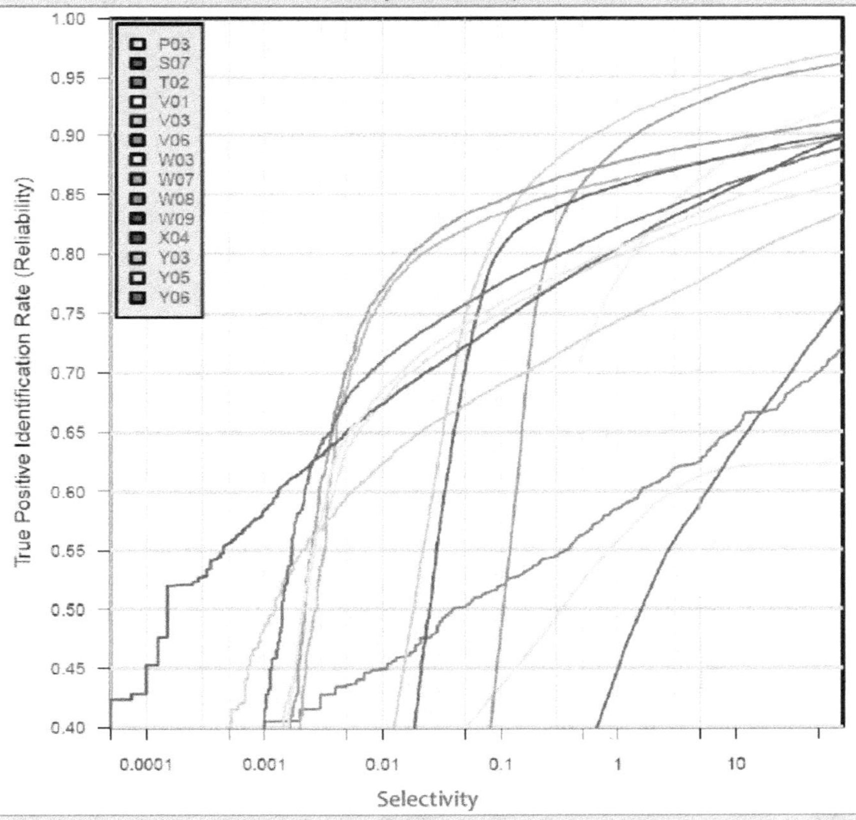

Number of searches with mate = 40000

Number of searches without mate = 40000

The vertical axis plots REL(T) = TPIR(R, T, L) where R=N=1600000 and L = 200.

The next two rows tabulate REL(T) at the threshold that gives SEL(T) = 0.5

SDK	V03	W08	V06	W07	W09	Y06	X04	Y05	W03	Y03	V01	T02	P03	S07
REL(T)	0.89	0.87	0.86	0.86	0.85	0.81	0.79	0.79	0.78	0.73	0.72	0.56	0.52	0.37

(b)

DOS / Natural (N = 1800000)

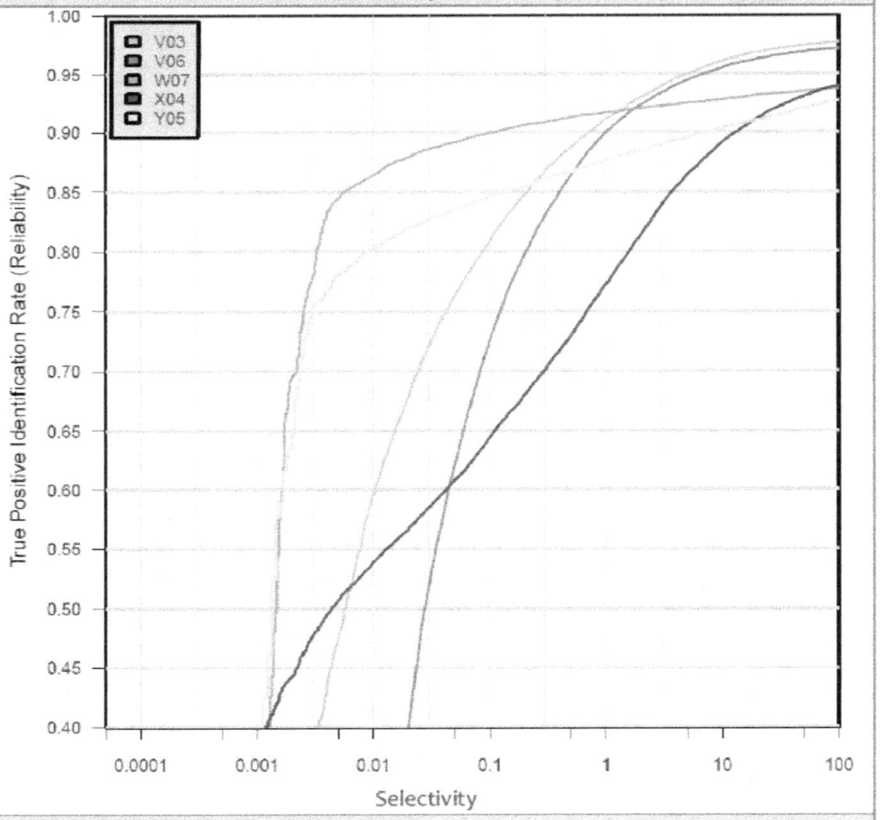

Number of searches with mate = 40000

Number of searches without mate = 40000

The vertical axis plots REL(T) = TPIR(R, T, L) where R=N=1800000 and L = 200.

The next two rows tabulate REL(T) at the threshold that gives SEL(T) = 0.5

SDK	W07	V03	Y05	Y06	X04
REL(T)	0.91	0.89	0.87	0.86	0.73

Demand driver: Face images are being collected in a number of civil and criminal applications [PINELLAS, JAPAN VISIT, US-VISIT, FBI]. The enrolled population increases with time. The number of subjects enrolled in the US-VISIT system has increased from 12 to 110 million in the seven years to 2010. The likelihood that a biometric sample collected during a prior encounter will be found in a one-to-many search is a function of the population size because the chance of one or more false matches increases with the population size.

Prior work: The FRVT 2002 study reported open-set identification accuracy as a function of the size of the enrolled population. In addition, a number of unpublished studies of 1:N facial recognition performance have been conducted as parts of procurement processes [WAGGETT].

The degree to which results can be extrapolated to large populations is a subject of debate. The academic studies have modeled empirical data [HUBE], or made assumptions of binomial independence [BOLLE, GROTHER, SHERRAH] in empirical data. One study ambitiously used experimental results from a population in the hundreds to predict performance in the billions [WEIN]. Leading commercial providers have also aware of the need to quantitatively model scaling [FONDEUR, JAROSZ, MARTIN].

Experimental method: Identical to INVESTIGATION 1.

Results: The plots of Figure 7 show the increase in false negative identification rates (i.e. miss rates) for each class C SDK as the size of the enrolled LEO population increases. The text in the side panel explains the format in more detail. The overall result is that FNIR increases approximately linear with the logarithm of population size N. The topmost curve for the V03 panel shows that rank 1 recognition error rate in a population of 10000 is 0.031 rising to 0.077 for 1.6 million.   For the W08 SDK the curves are notably flatter: The miss rate at 10000 is 0.1 and rises to 0.13 at 1.6 million.

Conclusions: There is an approximate dependence of accuracy on log of the population size.   This is not an exact model.

The observed results have applicability for the LEO dataset at the population sizes used. For larger populations, either an empirical trial will be conducted, or careful extrapolation will be needed to estimate performance.

Figure 7 – LEO Identification accuracy dependence on population size

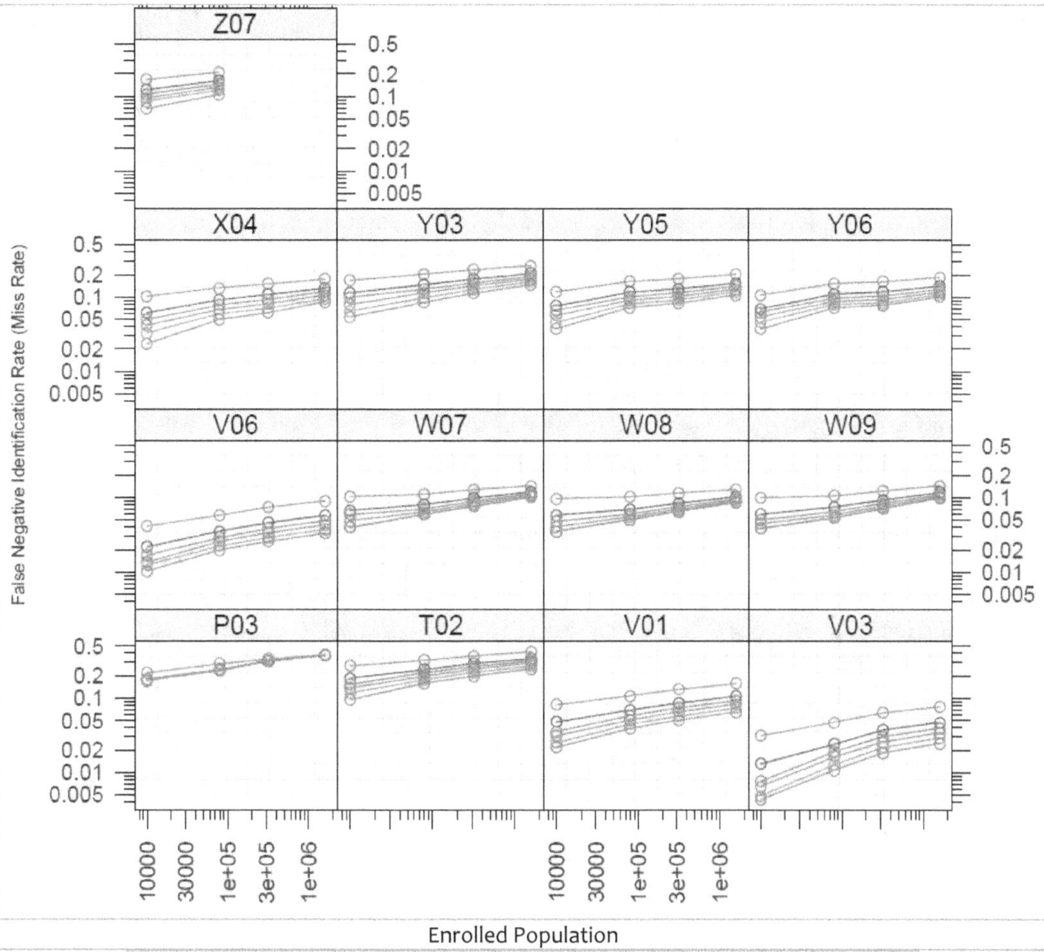

Each panel shows plots of hit rate versus enrolled population size for ranks 1, 10, 20, 50, 100, and 200. In each case the uppermost trace corresponds to Rank 1 Miss Rate – the proportion of searches for which the mate is not at rank 1. The population sizes run on a log scale from 10000 through to 1600000.

Missing points generally correspond to software failure.

SDK	TPIR(1, N, 200)			
	N=10000	N=80000	N=320000	N=160000
P03	0.782	0.712	0.667	0.619
T02	0.730	0.678	0.631	0.581
V01	0.918	0.892	0.869	0.842
V03	0.969	0.953	0.936	0.923
V06	0.959	0.942	0.926	0.910
W07	0.897	0.889	0.873	0.856
W08	0.903	0.898	0.885	0.872
W09	0.900	0.895	0.878	0.855
X04	0.898	0.866	0.849	0.826
Y03	0.833	0.796	0.767	0.736
Y05	0.882	0.837	0.824	0.798
Y06	0.893	0.847	0.839	0.815
Z07	0.833	0.789		

The Table quantifies True Positive Identification Rate, at rank 1 for four enrolled population sizes.

This is 1 minus the quantity graphed above:
FNIR = 1 – TPIR.

INVESTIGATION 4. *Dependence on rank*

What are the chances of finding a mate far down the candidate list?

Driver: In an investigational mode, a face recognition algorithm is used to provide a list of candidates to an examiner. The search image may have an enrolled mate, in which case the examiner may confirm the identity at some rank, or there may be no prior encounter of the individual, in which case the examiner would traverse and stop after finding no mates.

Experimental method: Identical to INVESTIGATION 1.

Results: Figure 8 re-plots the data of Figure 7 to show the dependence on rank. Each panel shows the dependence of hit rate on rank for a particular class C, one-to-many, SDK. The rank axis runs from 1 to 200 on a logarithmic scale. For any given population size, false negative identification rates exhibit an approximately linear dependence on the logarithm of the rank. While 200 candidates were requested, some systems (e.g. W07) returned candidate lists of length 200 for which the last 100 entries were zero. This produces a flat cumulative match characteristic. This may have occurred because the search algorithm is more efficient when fewer candidates are returned.

For some SDKs, FNIR decreases more rapidly with rank. This is especially true in smaller populations. This dependency was observed in the first CMC of Figure 5. Face identification algorithms which "front-load" a candidate list with mates offer workload benefits as discussed below.

Conclusions: As with other biometrics, accuracy of facial recognition implementations varies greatly across the industry. Absent other performance or economic parameters, users should prefer the most accurate algorithm. Note, however, that the results of this section are entirely rank-based – the CMC computations ignore score information. This befits use of face recognition in the investigational mode in which an examiner is willing to traverse candidate lists looking for mates. Subsequent investigations in this report consider threshold-based metrics appropriate for identification mode applications. There, the leading algorithms are different from those listed above.

Note that the absolute values of identification accuracy will always depend on the dataset used, specifically to the properties of the images in use. In particular this study includes some residual non-frontal images that eluded detection during the data preparation phase. These images include some 90-degree profiles, and, somewhat more frequently, images in which the face is at a 45 or 60 degree yaw angle to the camera. These images usually cause complete recognition failure and depress overall error rates.

Figure 8 – LEO identification miss rate versus rank.

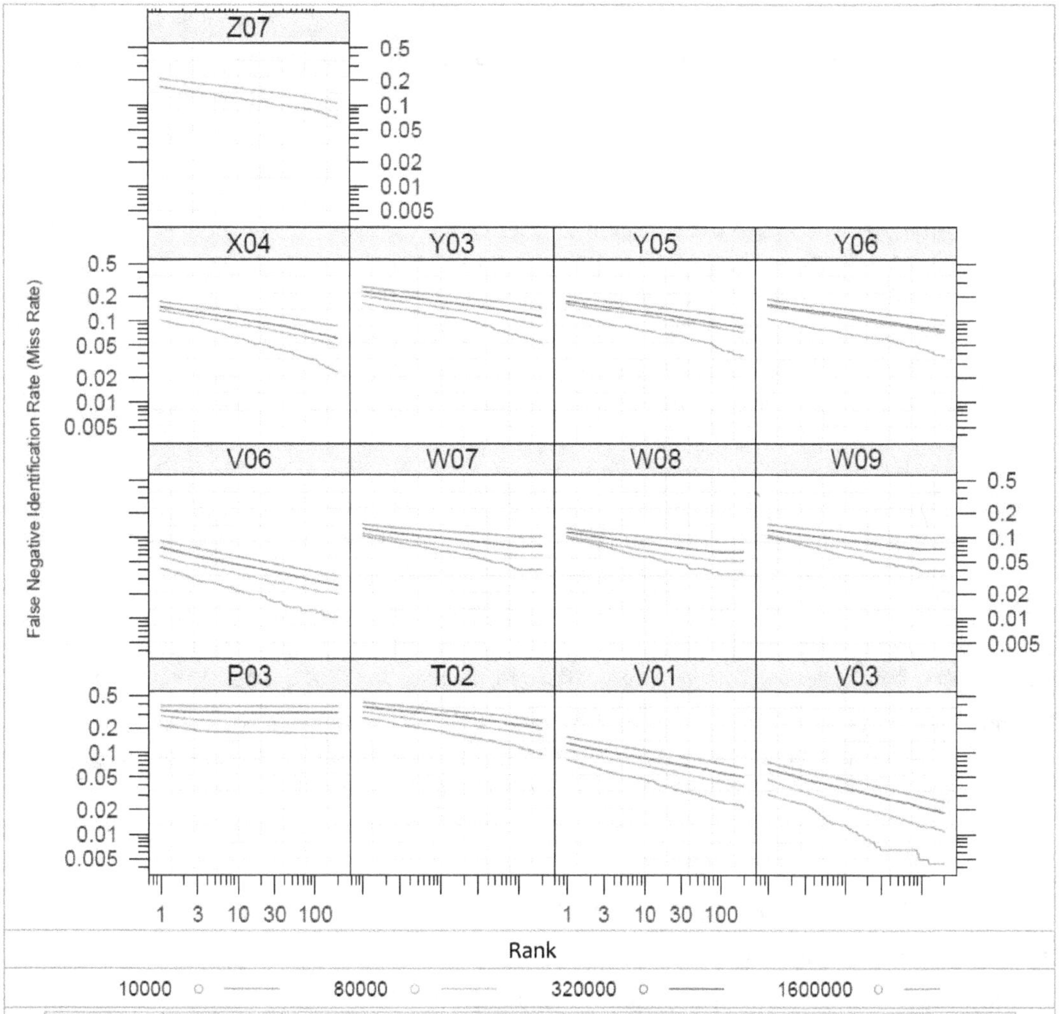

SDK	CMC(1)	CMC(10)	CMC(100)	
P03	0.619	0.623	0.623	
T02	0.581	0.665	0.730	
V01	0.842	0.893	0.926	The tabulated values are 1 – minus the false
V03	0.923	0.953	0.971	negative identification rates graphed above,
V06	0.910	0.942	0.962	i.e. CMC(R) = TPIR(R, 1600000, 200) for R = {
W07	0.856	0.881	0.898	1, 10, 100 }
W08	0.872	0.898	0.913	
W09	0.855	0.883	0.901	
X04	0.826	0.868	0.904	
Y03	0.736	0.793	0.839	
Y05	0.798	0.846	0.881	
Y06	0.815	0.859	0.891	

Workload implications: In a law enforcement scenario, for example, a human examiner might review the candidates returned in an identification search. Typically the examiner would compare each candidate with the search image starting with the highest scoring candidate and proceeding in descending order of similarity score. The examiner would stop early if he is able to positively confirm a mate. In this case, an expression for the total workload associated with resolving candidate lists of length K is derived as follows.

— The examiner will always inspect the first ranked image.   Num reviewed = 1

- The examiner will inspect the fraction of candidates not found at rank 1.   Num reviewed = 1-CMC(1)
- The examiner will inspect the fraction of candidates not found at rank 1 or 2.   Num reviewed = 1-CMC(2)

Etc. Thus if the examiner will stop at after a maximum of K candidates the expected number of candidate reviews is

$$M(K) = 1 + (1\text{-}CMC(1)) + (1\text{-}CMC(2) + ... + (1\text{-}CMC(K\text{-}1))$$
$$= K - \sum CMC(r) \text{ where the sum runs from } 1 \le r \le K\text{-}1$$

Equation 7

A recognition algorithm that front-loads the cumulative match characteristic will offer reduced workload for the examiner. This workload is defined only over the searches for which a mate exists. In the cases where there truly is no mate, the examiner would review all K candidates. Thus, if the proportion of searches for which a mate does exist is β, which in the law enforcement context would be the recidivism rate, the full expression for workload becomes:

$$M(K) = \beta (K - \sum CMC(r)) + (1 - \beta) K$$
$$= K - \beta \sum CMC(r) \text{ where the sum runs from } 1 \le r \le K\text{-}1$$

Equation 8

Figure 9 shows the dependence of M(K) as a function of K, for each class C identification SDK operating on LEO images. The text in the side panel explains each plot in more detail. Importantly we restrict the analysis to the case where there is always a mate, i.e. $\beta = 1$. This is done because the goal is to compare algorithms. However, note that if $\beta < 1$, examiners will have to review more candidates than are plotted here.

The plots show that if an examiner is willing to review, say, K = 60 candidates, then the expected number of candidates actually needing review will often be fewer than 10. For the V03 SDK the number is about 3.

Cost implications: The above expressions for examiner workload could be multiplied by suitable time and salary factors to estimate cost. Such a cost formulation should be extended to capture the cost of missing a mate altogether - This is a societal cost of failing to find a mate in the first K candidates.

Conclusions: The use of a face recognition system can dramatically decrease workload on a human examiner. The expected number of candidates before a mate is found is a useful performance metric for identification systems.

Assumptions: This workload model assumes the following:

- The candidates are reviewed serially, not all at once in a large screen GUI, for example.
- The candidates are searched in decreasing order of similarity score.
- The time taken to confirm or exclude a candidate is independent of the rank of the candidate.
- The time taken to confirm or exclude a candidate is independent of population size. This is potentially incorrect since identification in a very large population will produce candidates more similar to the search sample, than in smaller populations.
- Examiners will stop after confirming a mate.
- The database is correctly consolidated such that the number of mates is zero or one.
- Examiners always find a mate if it is present, and examiners do not assign a wrong mate. Particularly that examiner success is independent of β. Effects of fatigue and boredom have been reported when β is very low [GREATHOUSE].
- Scores are ignored and score thresholds are not applied.

Figure 9 – Workload implications of LEO cumulative match performance

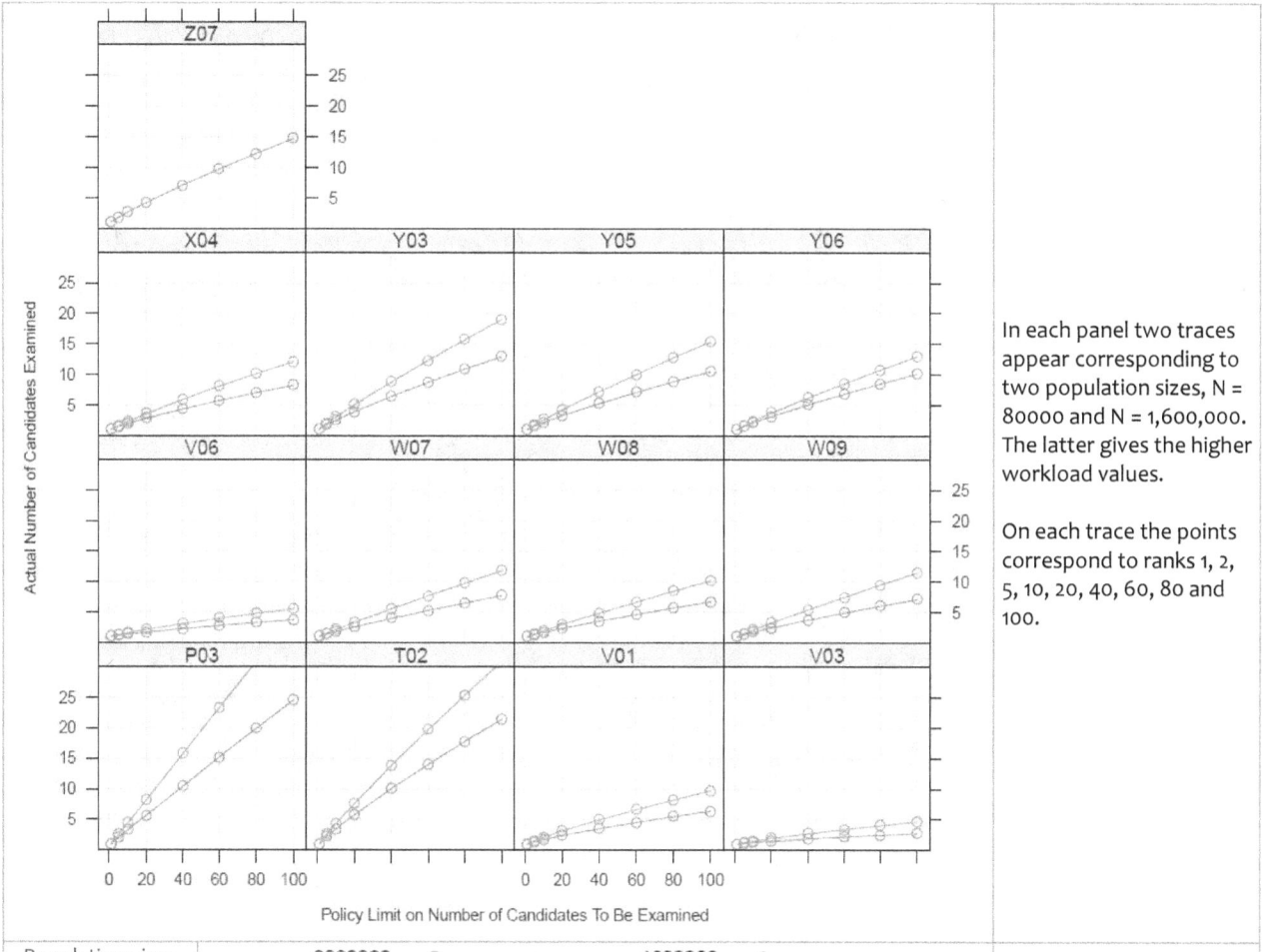

In each panel two traces appear corresponding to two population sizes, N = 80000 and N = 1,600,000. The latter gives the higher workload values.

On each trace the points correspond to ranks 1, 2, 5, 10, 20, 40, 60, 80 and 100.

Population sizes: 0080000 ○ ——— 1600000 ○ ———

INVESTIGATION 5. *Impostor distribution stability*

Selectivity is defined above as the number of false matches produced in a search against an operational database. If future photographs with different image properties are searched against this database, does selectivity change?

Demand driver: The operating threshold of a biometric system is set to meet some accuracy criterion such as a selectivity requirement.

Prior work: Most of the academic literature addresses improvement of Type 1 error rates such as better hit rates. The primary performance metrics are 1:1 FNMR at fixed FMR, and closet-set CMC. The importance of a stable impostor distribution is little discussed.

Experimental method: For four different providers' algorithms, V, W, X and Y, the identical candidate lists used INVESTIGATIONS 1 and 2, were analyzed as follows. ROCs were plotted for DOS/Natural and LEO on the same graph. For a small set of selectivities between 0.01 and 10, the thresholds that give those selectivities on the LEO dataset were computed. This computation uses only searches without mates. If for algorithm, i, the thresholds are T_i, then the point $(SEL(T_i), REL(T_i))_{LEO}$ is joined to $(SEL(T_i), REL(T_i))_{DOS}$ with a grey line.

NOTE: The experiment did not enroll LEO and DOS images together into a single database. This would have supported the use of score normalization.

Results: ROCs are shown in Figure 10. With DOS data, all algorithms give generally higher reliability than with LEO data. Three of the four algorithms give better selectivity also. The one exception is the X04 algorithm which produces many more candidates above a fixed threshold value with the DOS / Natural imagery than with LEO.

A desirable property for a biometric system is to have a stationary impostor distribution. This allows a threshold to be set so that false match statistics are known and controlled. This is difficult if the properties of the images are unknown. The alternative is to set the threshold for the specific database. The approach to threshold setting is out-of-scope of this test.

The algorithms were informed of the kind of the images being used. Thus each DOS / Natural image was tagged with a label "visa", and each LEO image with the label "mugshot". The SDK could, in principle, invoke completely different template generation and matching algorithms for the two image variants. This might necessitate setting of database-specific thresholds.

Figure 10 - Reliability and selectivity at a fixed threshold

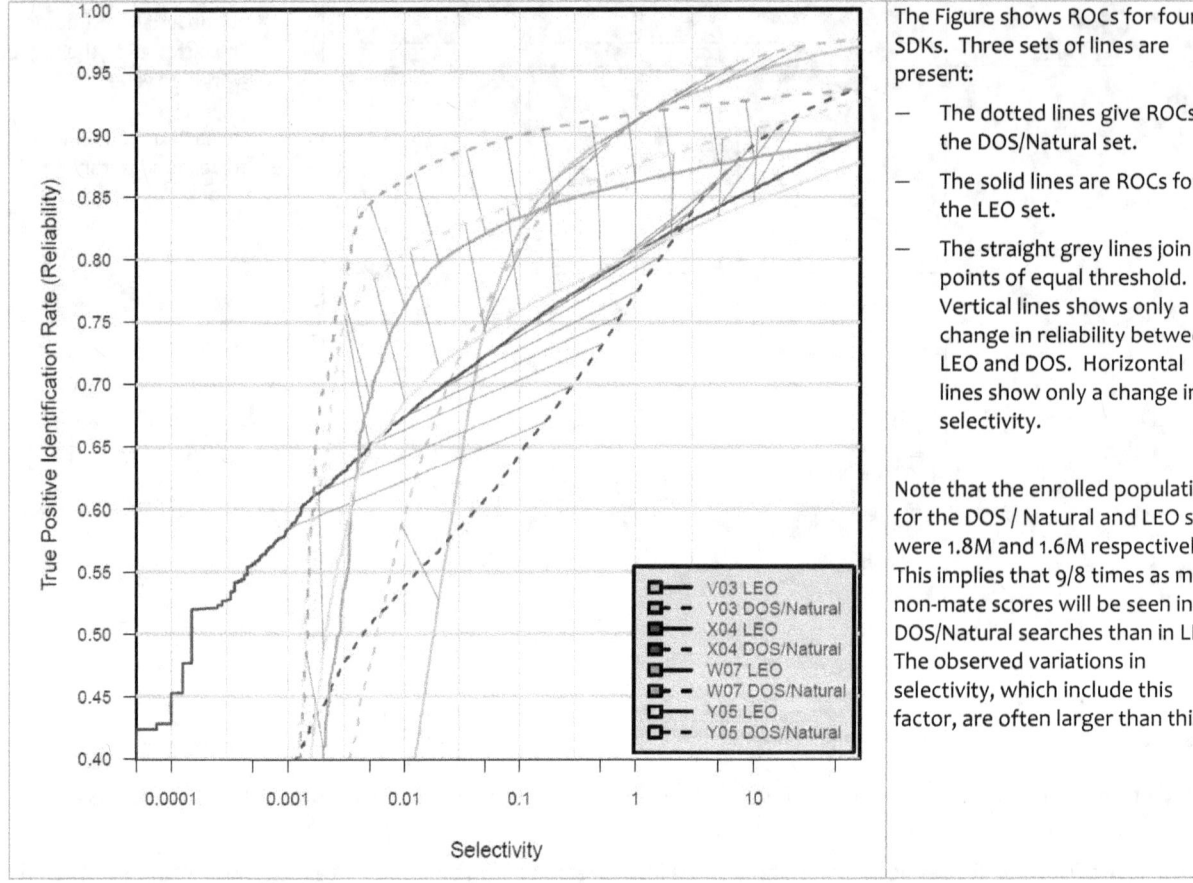

The Figure shows ROCs for four SDKs. Three sets of lines are present:

- The dotted lines give ROCs for the DOS/Natural set.

- The solid lines are ROCs for the LEO set.

- The straight grey lines join points of equal threshold. Vertical lines shows only a change in reliability between LEO and DOS. Horizontal lines show only a change in selectivity.

Note that the enrolled populations for the DOS / Natural and LEO sets were 1.8M and 1.6M respectively. This implies that 9/8 times as many non-mate scores will be seen in the DOS/Natural searches than in LEO. The observed variations in selectivity, which include this factor, are often larger than this.

Conclusions: Algorithms exhibit variation in selectivity (the number of non-mates returned in a search) when a fixed threshold is used on two different enrollment databases. Thus, depending on the application requirements and the algorithm, the threshold may not be portable across datasets, and may need to be calibrated using a set of non-mated searches.

INVESTIGATION 6. *Search duration*
And does the time to identify scale linearly with the size of the enrolled population?

Demand driver: In most deployments, the enrolled population increases over time. This may be a continuous process or the result of merging separate datasets. If the database doubles in size, does the search time? This has major implications for planning, and system cost.

Prior work: There are no publically reported tests in operational populations. There is a large and mature literature on fast search algorithms, although most of this is outside of the biometric arena. The term fast refers to algorithms for which average search time increases better-than-linearly with population size N, for example as log N.

Experimental method: Calls to the one-to-many search function were made on a dedicated computer. The computer was not running any other processes except those back-grounded as part of the operating system. The durations are measured by wrapping the elemental identify_template function [MBE-API, Table 27] in a wall time counter[7]. The measurements do not include disk access unless the SDK under test elected to access enrollment or configuration data during a search – this is not necessary because the API supported initialization prior to searching.

The MBE-STILL test plan formally stated the durations of Table 18 as limits on the core elemental functions of the SDKs. The times were stated as 90-th percentiles.

Table 18 – Processing time limits in milliseconds

	1	2	3	4	5
Function		1:1 verification without enrollment database	1:1 verification with enrollment database	1:N identification	Pose conformance estimation
Feature extraction enrollment		1000 (1 core)	1000 (1 core)	1000 (1 core)	
Feature extraction for verification or identification		1000 (1 core)	1000 (1 core)	1000 (1 core)	
Verification		5 (1 core)	10 (1 core)	NA	500 (1 core)
Identification of one search image against 1,000,000 single-image MULTIFACE records.		NA	NA	10000 (16 cores) or 160000 (1 core)	

In identification trials, the SDK was permitted to use the available hardware as it saw fit. For, the implementation could elect to start any number of threads [1,16] and this could be varied dynamically and as a function of N.

Table 19 – Adjustment of search duration estimates by number of cores used

SDK Identifier	Number of cores used by SDK in a search	For a search of duration, T, the time reported by NIST	Remarks
Vxx Txx	1	T / 16	The divisor is applied because 16 searches can be executed independently on the standard hardware used in this test. Operationally this is unrealistic unless 16 separate search transactions are actually outstanding. Otherwise the hardware is wasted.
All others	16	T	These implementations use threads to fully utilize the available cores hardware for a single search.

Duration measurements were made by executing searches involving mates and non-mates in a random order. The search population was N = 10000, 80000, 320000, and 1600000. Only LEO images were used.

The estimates reported below are median values estimated over 1000 searches for which a mate exists, and 1000 searches for which a mate does not exist.

---

[7] The standard "C" call get_time_of_day() function has resolution of 16ms on windows hosts but microseconds under linux.

Results: Figure 11 shows the duration, T, of a search as a function of enrolled population size, N, for the LEO images. In each panel there are two traces, one each for searches with and without mates. The median times in these two cases are so close together that the traces lie directly on top of each other, and only one trace is visible[8]. The functional form in most cases is an approximately straight line on a log-log plot. This observation, $\log T = a \log N + b$, corresponds to a power-law form $T = cN^a$ where the constant $b = \log c$ determines the intercept on the observed plot, and the constant a is the slope.

For the V-series SDKs the dependence is linear (a ~ 1). For the W-series SDKs the scaling is better (the coefficient "a" is as low as 0.1). However, while the V-series SDKs are absolutely faster, this only applies for populations in the millions. In the tens of millions the W-series SDKs would be faster unless algorithmic changes were made.

Figure 11 – Duration of LEO identification searches

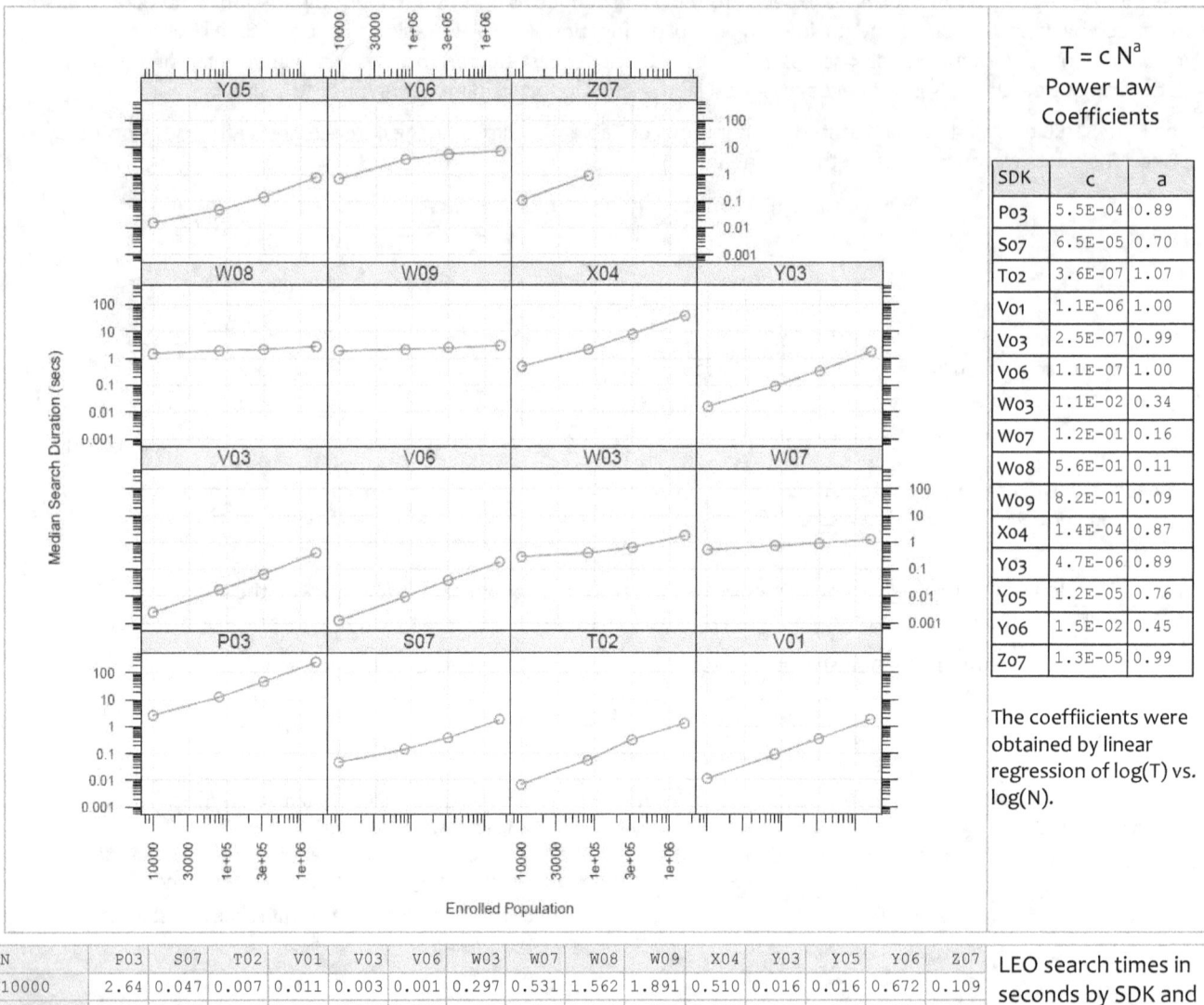

$T = c N^a$
Power Law Coefficients

SDK	c	a
P03	5.5E-04	0.89
S07	6.5E-05	0.70
T02	3.6E-07	1.07
V01	1.1E-06	1.00
V03	2.5E-07	0.99
V06	1.1E-07	1.00
W03	1.1E-02	0.34
W07	1.2E-01	0.16
W08	5.6E-01	0.11
W09	8.2E-01	0.09
X04	1.4E-04	0.87
Y03	4.7E-06	0.89
Y05	1.2E-05	0.76
Y06	1.5E-02	0.45
Z07	1.3E-05	0.99

The coefficients were obtained by linear regression of log(T) vs. log(N).

N	P03	S07	T02	V01	V03	V06	W03	W07	W08	W09	X04	Y03	Y05	Y06	Z07	
10000	2.64	0.047	0.007	0.011	0.003	0.001	0.297	0.531	1.562	1.891	0.510	0.016	0.016	0.672	0.109	LEO search times in
80000	12.31	0.141	0.056	0.089	0.017	0.009	0.391	0.734	1.953	2.188	2.170	0.094	0.047	3.656	0.875	seconds by SDK and
320000	47.07	0.375	0.322	0.357	0.067	0.038	0.641	0.921	2.141	2.437	8.181	0.344	0.141	5.718		population size, N.
1600000	238.9	1.750	1.334	1.793	0.394	0.177	1.750	1.234	2.781	3.001	39.70	1.765	0.766	7.141		

Conclusions: Search durations scale approximately as a power of the database size. The coefficients are dependent on the algorithm. There are approximately two orders of magnitude difference in the search durations measured for the two most accurate algorithms.

---

[8] This result differs from some applications [MINEXII] where matching times depend on whether a genuine or impostor comparison is being conducted.

MBE-STILL REPORT	P = PITTPATT	R = SURREY U.	S = TSINGHUA U.	T = TOSHIBA	U = DALIAN U.	PAGE 34 OF 61
PARTICIPANT KEY	V = NEC	W = L1 IDENTITY	X = COGNITEC	Y = SAGEM	Z = NEUROTECHNOLOGY	

INVESTIGATION 7. *Verification accuracy*
Face recognition is increasingly being used in access control systems. What is the accuracy?

Demand driver: The accuracy of the core verification algorithm is an important part of a face-based identity verification algorithm. However, unlike the case for identification, a recognition transaction may consist of several captures and comparisons, with the possibility to provide feedback to the user and to re-acquire a photograph. These aspects will produce better transactional accuracy. Identification systems, often incorporating backend matching systems, do not benefit from transactional cooperation of the user. Nevertheless accuracy of the core algorithm is influential on outcome.

Prior work: One-to-one verification has been measured in innumerable academic studies, and also in larger scale independent testing efforts [FRVT2002, FRVT2006].

Experimental method: Two datasets were employed. Forty thousand subjects randomly drawn from the LEO set formed the enrollment set against which 9240 individuals were verified. These comparisons produced the genuine scores. Single images from a further, disjoint, population of 10000 individuals were used to execute impostor comparisons. The second dataset, DOS / HCINT, was used in exactly the same manner as in prior NIST tests [FRVT2002, FRVT2006]. Twelve sets of 3000 persons were compared with 2 images of those persons to produce 12 times 6000 genuine scores. Those same persons were then compared with individuals from the next, disjoint, 3000-person set. This produced 18 million true impostor scores. All the persons had K=1 enrollment samples.

Figure 12 – Verification accuracies of class A algorithms.

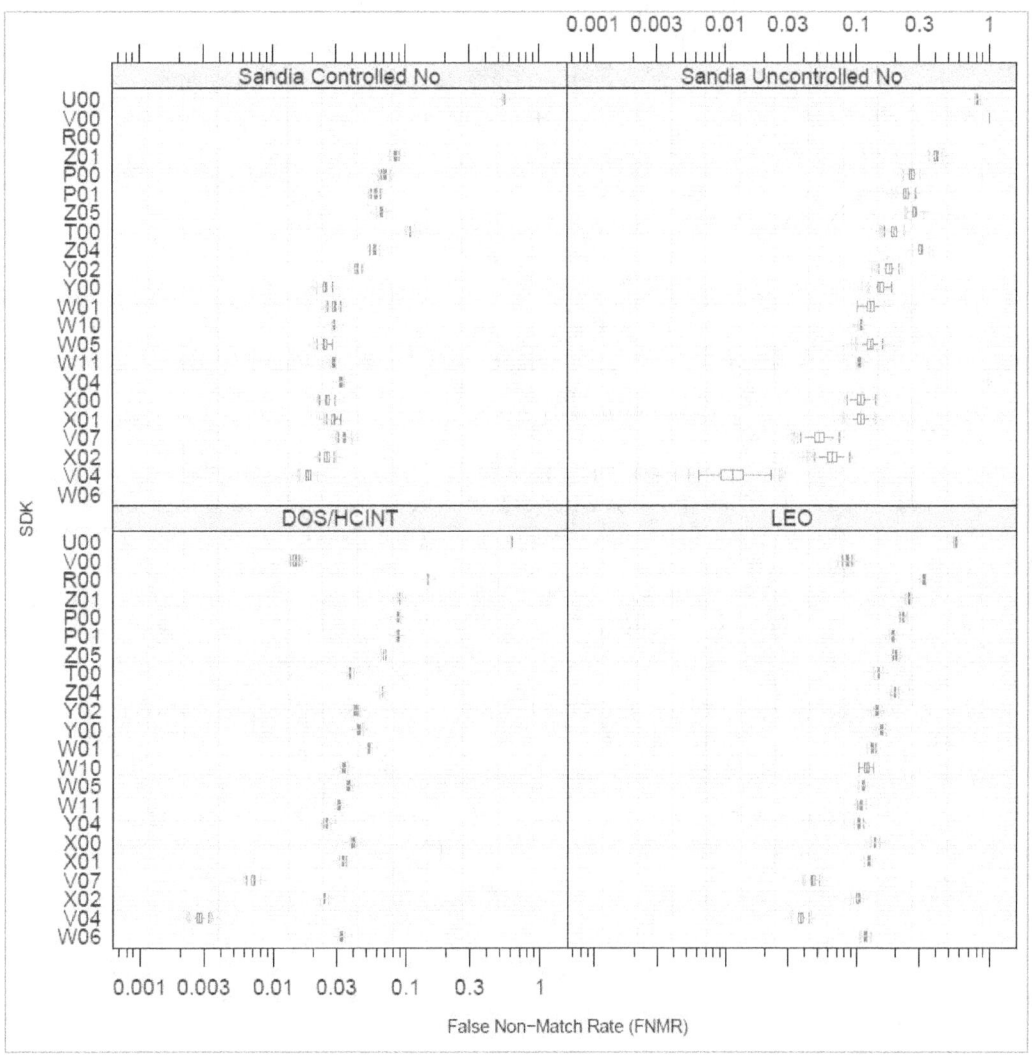

Results: Figure 12 shows boxplots of FNMR for one-to-one verification accuracy for the DOS/HCINT and LEO datasets. FNMR is stated at FMR = 0.001. The threshold was set to give this FMR for each particular SDK and dataset. All the SDKs are class A, running without an enrollment database.

There is an order of magnitude variation in FNMR between verification algorithms running on the LEO images. For the DOS / HCINT images this increases to two orders of magnitude.

Conclusions: Error rates on DOS/HCINT have reduced dramatically in the last 8 years. In 2002, the best FNMR values at FMR = 0.001 was 0.2. This reduced to 0.026 in FRVT 2006, and to below 0.003 for the leading SDK in this test. The DOS images are overly compressed and exhibit some too-close-to-camera distortion effects.

INVESTIGATION 8. *Verification accuracy with and without an enrollment database*
Face verification can proceed by comparing a live capture with a face stored on an identity credential, or by comparing the live capture with an entry in an enrolled database. Is accuracy the same?

Demand driver: Face verification applications are deployed with and without a database of enrolled identities:

— The e-Passport gate task compares an image from height-adjustable cameras with the ISO/IEC 19794-5:2005 image read from the DG2 structure of the ICAO 9303 passport. There is purely comparison of images from the passport holder: There is no possibility to compare the image with other images of passport holders[9].

— In a physical access control system (e.g. time-and-attendance, or a gymnasium access), all users could be enrolled and their templates maintained as an enrollment database. One might be selected via PIN or card presentation.

The use and maintenance of a face database is sometimes contra-indicated by communication constraints and by privacy policy considerations.

Prior work: To support the use of normalization across the enrollment dataset, the FRVT 2002 test allowed application of a post-processing function to the N scores produced by comparing a verification image with images in the enrollment set. The FRVT 2006 test explicitly solicited SDKs with and without normalization. In both cases, accuracy benefits were documented.

Experimental method: Using a fixed set of 40000 enrollment subjects, both genuine and impostor verification trials were conducted using class B SDKs. The class A implementations execute purely independent comparisons of template pairs. The class B implementations execute a comparison of a verification template with a specific enrolled identity and may internally compare just those two templates, or may undertake to utilize the remaining entries of the enrollment database in some effective way.

Results: Figure 13a shows FNMR at FMR = 0.001 for some providers who shipped both class A vs class B SDKs. Class A performance is represented by solid lines and class B performance by dotted lines. Curves are color coded by provider. False non-match rates at select false match rates are labeled. The Class B algorithms for V05/V08 produce identical scores to their V04/V07 class A counterparts. Thus, in the figure the dotted and solid line performance curves follow the same paths, with the result that only the solid lines are visible. This implies that the Vxx implementations do not perform any normalization across the enrollment dataset. For the P and X algorithms, the class B algorithms produce lower error rates than their corresponding class A algorithms.

The barplot in Figure 13b shows how class B algorithms compare to their corresponding class A algorithms. The class B algorithms tend to perform better, but there are cases where people correctly matched by the class A algorithm are missed by the corresponding class B algorithm (indicated by the light-red bars in the figure).

Conclusions: The Class B algorithms from provider V give identical scores to their class A counterparts. The X03 algorithm performed better than X02. However, the best performing algorithms (V02 and V05) do not perform any normalization across the enrollment dataset.

---

[9] A face recognition installation might include an internal normalization dataset. Such a set is unlikely to optimally represent the population of images that the e-Passport holder is presenting.

Figure 13 – LEO Verification accuracy with and without enrollment datasets

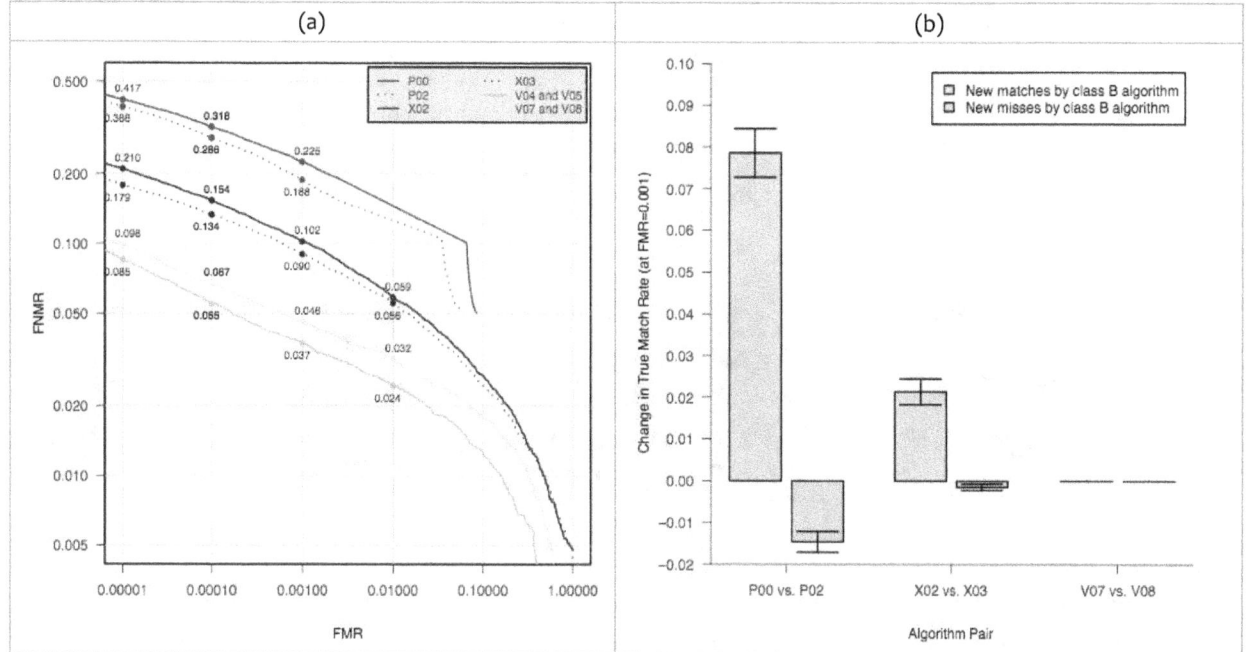

INVESTIGATION 9. *Exploiting all prior images*

If a facial recognition implementation is provided with the complete set of historical images of a person, does accuracy improve?

Demand driver: Many operational applications include collection and enrollment of biometric data from subjects on more than one occasion. This may be done on a regular basis, as might occur in passport issuance for example, or irregularly, as might happen in a criminal recidivist situation. In any case, the question arises whether accuracy can be improved if the face recognition implementation is allowed to exploit all prior images. This contrasts with typical practice in which the image from the most recent encounter replaces prior enrollments.

The number of images per person will depend on the application area:

— In civil identity credentialing (e.g. passports, driving licenses) the images will be acquired approximately uniformly over time (e.g. five years for a Canadian passport). While the distribution of dates for such images of a person might be assumed uniform, a number of factors might undermine this assumption[10].

— In criminal applications the number of images would depend on the number of arrests[11]. The distribution of dates for arrest records for a person (i.e. the recidivism distribution) has been modeled using the exponential distribution, but is recognized to be more complicated.

Fundamental concept: This document defines a template to be the result of applying feature extraction to a set of $K \geq 1$ images and merging the results. That is, a template contains the features extracted from one or more images, not generally just one. This is depicted in Table 20. The template is a single proprietary block of data. There are no facial template standards.

---

[10] For example, a person might skip applying for a passport for one cycle (letting it expire). In addition, a person might submit identical images (from the same photography session) to consecutive passport applications at five year intervals.

[11] A number of distributions have been considered to model recidivism, see for example [BLUMENSTEIN]. ``Random parameter stochastic process models of criminal careers.'' In Blumstein, Cohen, Roth & Visher (Eds.), Criminal Careers and Career Criminals, Washington, D.C.: National Academy of Sciences Press, 1986.

All verification comparisons and identification searches operate on such combined templates. This delegates the responsibility for fusion to the technology provider. This implies that end-users and system integrators should procure multi-image fusion capability; they should not implement this themselves.

Prior work: Use of multiple images per person has been shown to elevate accuracy over a single image [FRVT2002b]. While there are many academic publications in this area [MIN], many refer to the recognition-from-video problem which benefits from an ability to track the subject through time, and the use of single sensor. This covers early to late-stage integration strategies [SHAKNAROVICH]. The former is typically template-level fusion in which an algorithm might internally fuse K feature sets into a single representation. In the case of score-level fusion, the algorithm might match against the K feature sets separately and, for example, take the sum-score [KITTLER] or maximum score.

Table 20 – Uses of K images of a MEDS dataset subject for testing

Image	Enrolled images					Search (aka probe)
Encounter	1	2	3	...	K-1	K
Capture time	T_1	T_2	T_3		T_{K-1}	T_K
Role **RECENT**	Not used	Not used	Not used	...	1 image enrolled	Probe
Role **LIFETIME**	N-1 images provided to SDK together and enrolled into a single template					Probe

Experimental method: Some of the proposed datasets includes K > 2 images per person for some subjects. This affords the possibility to model a recognition scenario in which a new image of a person is compared against all prior images[12]. We ran two tests. The first shows the effect of using multiple images in a verification scenario. The second breaks out identification performance by the number of images enrolled. These are described as follows.

— Identification: The data and identification trials are identical to that used in investigations 1-4. The analysis is threshold based.

  Verification: The verification test uses a population of 40000 persons from the LEO set. A fixed disjoint set of 10000 persons, one image per person was used to generate 400M impostor scores. A fixed set of 9240 persons was used to generate genuine scores. These were the most recent images of the enrolled subjects[13]. In the case where multiple images per person were enrolled, the total number of enrolled images was 45395. The method by which the face recognition implementation exploits multiple images is not regulated: The test seeks to evaluate vendor provided technology for multi-instance fusion. This departs from some prior NIST tests in which NIST executed fusion algorithms ([e.g. [FRVT2002b], and sum score fusion, for example, [MINEX]).

---

[12] For example, if a banned driver applies for a driving license under a new name, and the local driving license authority maintains a driving license system in which all previous driving license photographs are enrolled, then the fraudulent application might be detected if the new image matched any of the prior images. This example implies one (elemental) method of using the image history.

[13] To mimic operational reality, NIST intends to maintain a causal relationship between probe and enrolled images. This means that the enrolled images of a person will be acquired before all the images that comprise a probe.

Figure 14 – LEO Identification accuracy by number of prior encounters

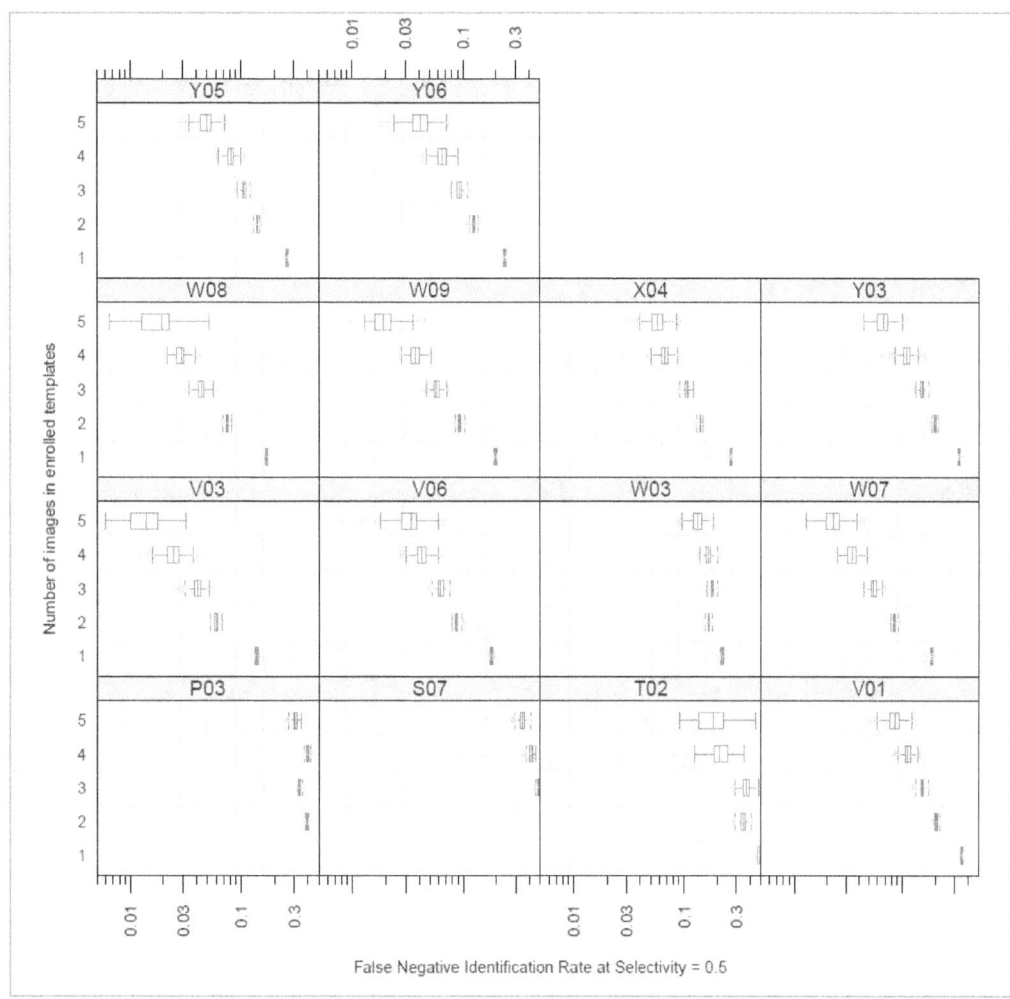

Results: Figure 14 shows identification accuracy broken out by the number of enrolled images per person. Specifically the plots show estimates of the FNIR(T) for persons enrolled with 1, 2, 3, 4 or 5 images, when the threshold T is set to produce a selectivity, SEL(T) = 0.5. Each boxplot summarizes 1000 bootstrap estimates of FNIR(T).

Some SDKs (P03, W03, for example) do not show accuracy gains from the use of multiple images. These SDKs may have elected to ignore all but the most recent, or the best enrollment image. Most SDKs do realize accuracy gains, and these are substantial: For SDKs W09 and V03, the FNIR values are between 5 and 10 times lower for persons enrolled with five images than with one.

The operational relevance of this result is dependent on the natural occurrence of multiple encounter data, the distribution of which is captured in the image counts of Table 6. To assess the overall effect we use verification results to quantify overall gains. Figure 15 gives boxplots of verification accuracies for 1:1 class A SDKs. Each boxplot summarizes 1000 bootstrap estimates of false non-match rate (FNMR) at a fixed false-match rate (FMR) of 0.001. The center of the box gives the median. There are two boxplots for each SDK. The first gives FNMR for the population when multiple enrolled images are used, i.e. K ≥ 1. The second gives FNMR when identically one image per person is enrolled, i.e K = 1.

Figure 15 – LEO Verification accuracy with and without multiple enrollment samples

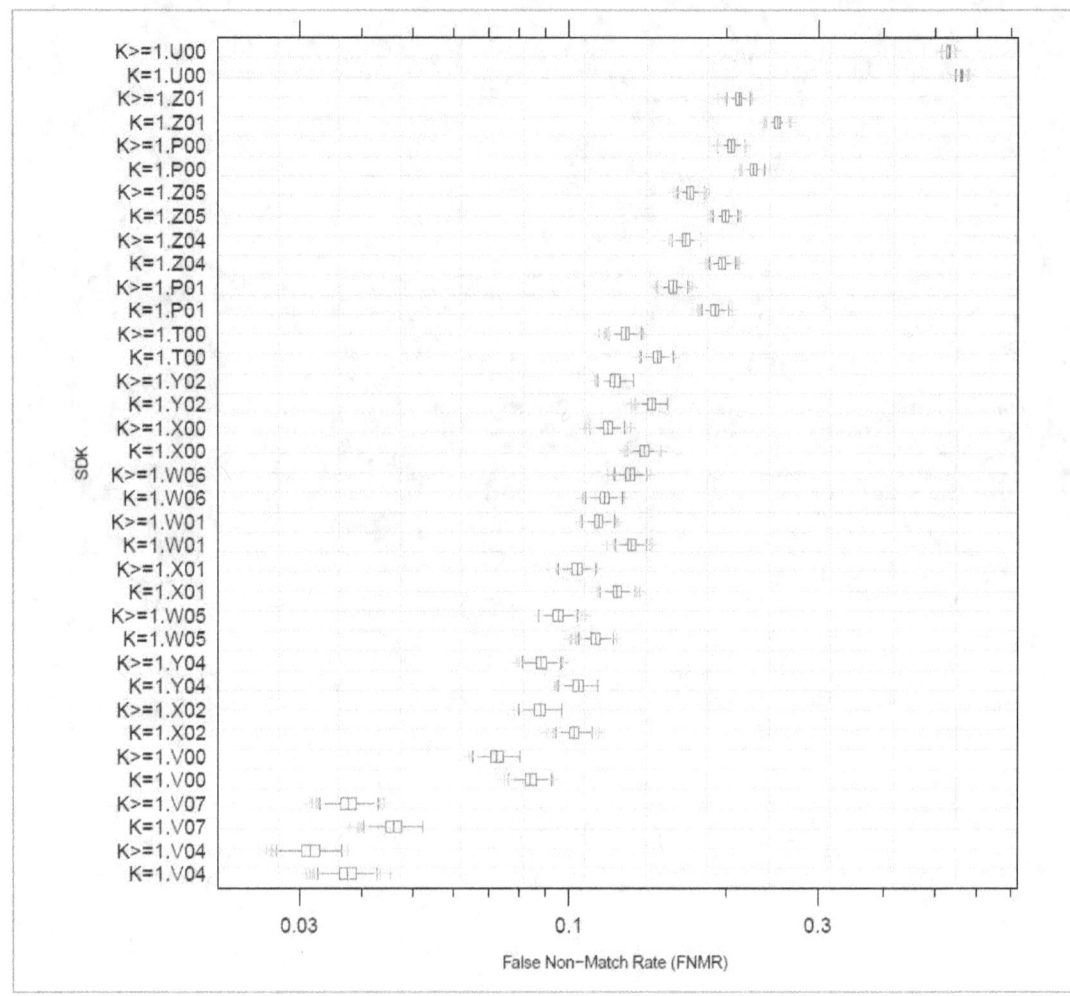

Results from verification trials using LEO images show that FNMR decreases for all SDKs. The improvements are significant. Importantly, the overall benefit observed here depends on the fraction of the enrolled population with multiple encounters in the enrollment database. In the LEO population, the fraction of subjects who have multiple enrollment images is about 14%. The use of multiple-encounter data is effective because any given image may exhibit defects that cause recognition failure.

Conclusions: When all prior images or a person are enrolled under one identity, accuracy improvements in both verification and identification trials are realized. The value of multiple images increases with the number of images. Some algorithms exploit the availability more than others. The overall operational impact is related to the distribution of the number of images per person. Subjects from the LEO dataset with multiple images are more likely to be identified in a subsequent search.

INVESTIGATION 10. *Exploiting all prior images: A false match hazard?*
So by enrolling multiple images of a person, there is an increase in hit rate, but is there also a greater chance that un-enrolled subjects will false match against such enrollments?

Demand driver: The prior section showed that most algorithms realize reductions in the Type I error rate by exploiting the lifetime image history. However, there is a possibility that subjects enrolled with multiple images may attract more false matches. An enrollee producing elevated false-match rates is known as a lamb in the biometric zoo

[DODDINGTON]. The face recognition algorithm, particularly its approach to fusion, is responsible for mitigating this risk.

Experimental method: As in prior investigation.

Results: Figure 16 shows, for each SDK, the selectivity associated with enrollees who have K=1, 2, 3, 4 and 5 LEO enrollment images in their template. The threshold is fixed to give an overall selectivity of 0.5. The desirable behavior is that selectivity is not a function of K. Also acceptable is that selectivity reduces with increasing K. The undesirable result an increase in selectivity because this would, depending on the application, give elevated workload to examiners.

Conclusions: The algorithms demonstrate benign false positive behavior when enrolling a person with k > 1 image.

Figure 16 – LEO Selectivity by number of prior encounters

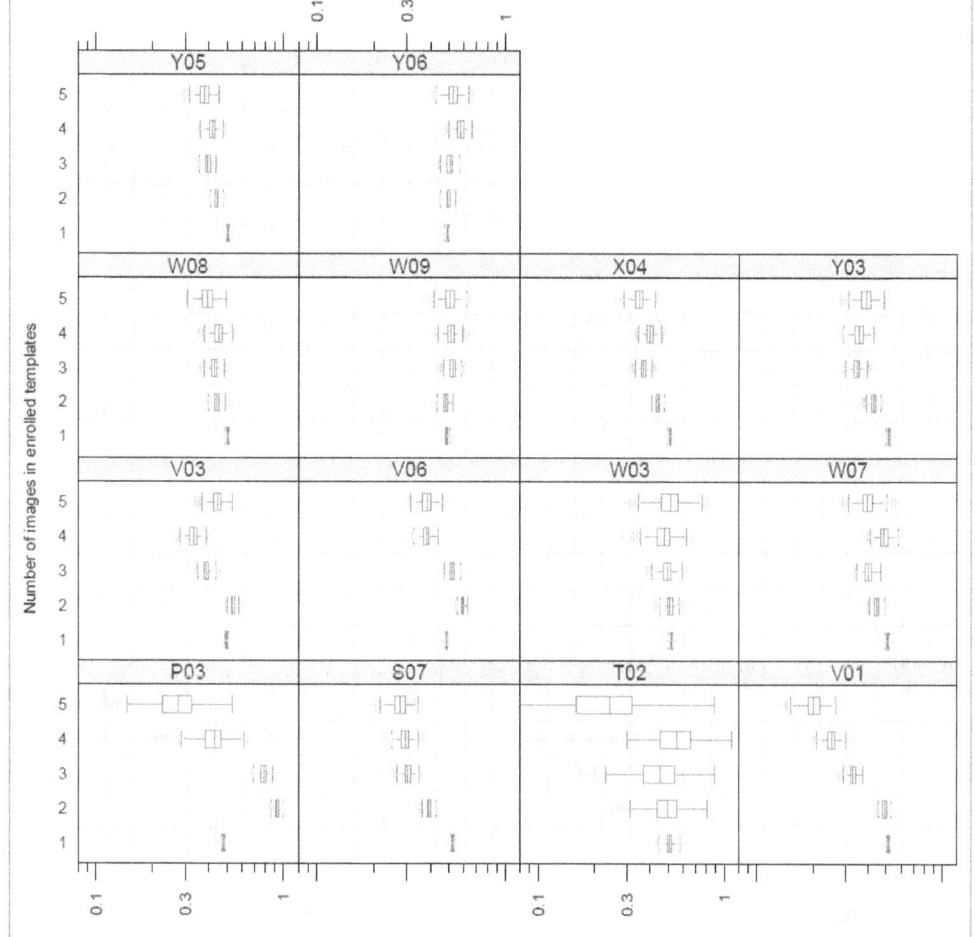

INVESTIGATION 11. *Evidentiary value*

Can face recognition algorithms be used to support a statement of the form, "the chance that these two faces come from the different subjects is less than one in ten thousand"?

Demand driver: All biometric access control systems require a calibration of the false match rate so that a threshold, T, can be set. A score exceeding the threshold might result in an undetected false acceptance. Likewise, in an identification application, a high score might trigger an investigation, typically involving human adjudication of the result. The threshold T is used to implement a decision policy. It will usually be set according to stated cost considerations, estimates of impostor likelihoods, and an empirical calibration of the recognition algorithm response.

The intention then is to set a threshold so that the chance of two different persons matching is actually less than an FMR requirement. In practice, while the threshold might be set on the basis of theoretical considerations, or on an ad hoc basis, it is in practically set empirically. Thus, a calibration exercise is undertaken: A particular facial recognition algorithm is used to compare many images from a large population of persons, and the empirical cumulative distribution function of the observed impostor scores, N(s), gives an estimate of the chance that images of different persons will reach a high value, s, via

$$P (s \mid impostor) = FMR(s) = 1 - N(s)$$

The use case is as follows. A laboratory is given two images and is asked do the images come from the same person. The lab passes the images through a one-to-one comparison engine to obtain a comparison score. If the score, s, is far above the mean of the observed impostor distribution, then the FMR(s) calibration might be considered as sufficient to assert that the chance we'd see this outcome from different persons is less than 1 part in a million, say. However, this is not true: FMR(s) is an estimate of the probability that two persons who are known to be different would generate a score greater than or equal to s. The more useful number, the posterior probability that the persons are different given the score is obtained via Bayes' rule:

$$P(impostor \mid s) \quad = \quad P(s \mid impostor) \; \frac{P(impostor)}{P(s)}$$

where P(Impostor) is the *prior* probability that an impostor event would even occur, and P(s) is the probability that a score, whether genuine or impostor, occurs. P(s) can be estimated from knowledge of the prior probabilities and from the results of a calibration trial: P(s) = P(s | impostor) P(impostor) + P (s | genuine) P(genuine). The prior probability P(impostor) = 1 – P(genuine) is obviously dependent on the domain of use and may not even be stable over time. When it is small, the posterior probability given by the last equation will be small even if FMR(s) is large.

The opposite is not true: a low score does not necessarily mean the images are of different persons. This arises because defective images produce low scores even in same-person comparisons. The term defective might mean low contrast, blurred, non-frontal pose, and exaggerated expression.

Table 21 – Interpretation of impostor scores

Score	Image properties	Supported conclusion
High	Good quality	Same person – but see the discussion of prior probabilities above, and the critical caveats below
High	Poor quality	This outcome should not occur
Low	Good quality and no sign of manipulation or evasive behavior	Different persons, typically, but see discussion of prior probabilities above
Low	Poor quality	Indeterminate

The actual reliability of the threshold will depend on the impostor distribution stability over the lifetime of the operation. However a number of factors may undermine the calibration. These include:

— Changes in the photometric and geometric properties of the images.

— Changes in the compression applied to the images.

— Changes in the demographics of the population.

— Changes in the ethnic mix of the population.

A very important caveat on this analysis is that the calibration method here is based on image corpora that do not include all photometric and geometric variants. For example, it does not include highly compressed images, taken with a flash, that exhibit fish-eye distortion. It is possible that such images, from truly different people, might give impostor scores much higher than those used to establish the calibrations here.

Experimental method: NIST used the class A SDKs to execute 400 million one-to-one comparisons of LEO images, and to use the resulting scores to compute empirical cumulative distribution functions.

Result: Figure 17 shows plots the right tail of one minus the empirical cumulative distribution function (ECDF) of the impostor distribution, i.e. they plot FMR against threshold, i.e. FMR(T). The vertical axis is logarithmic. The curves are uninteresting in the sense that they show the expected monotonic decrease of FMR with threshold. Their utility, however, is as calibration curves - they allow a user to set a threshold to target a particular FMR. The calibration is worthwhile only to the extent that the impostor distribution is stable for the lifetime of the operation.

Figure 17 – LEO False Match Rate calibration curves

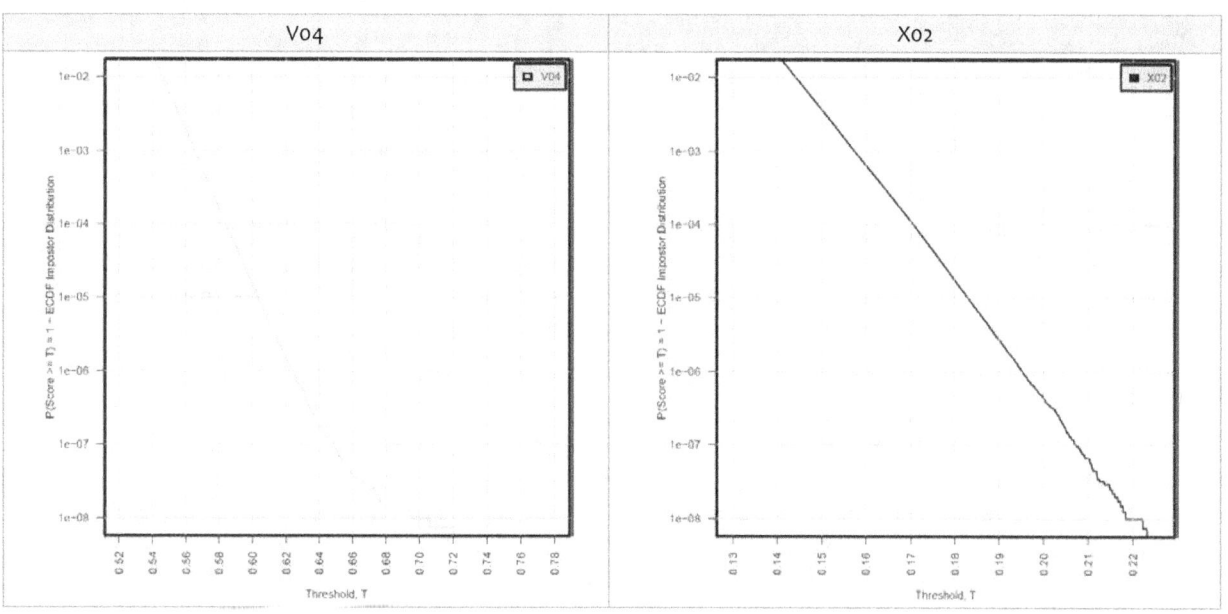

Conclusion: The calibration curve supports a statement of the form: "According to the automated face recognition calibration, the likelihood that this image pair come from different people is 1 part in 300,000". The method is applicable in identification scenarios if any given candidate from an identification search is compared with the hypothesized enrollment sample using the 1:1 SDK.

Caveats: The above results are subject to the following caveats and assumptions, and should be used with caution.

— **Algorithm effects.** The calibration may not apply if the face recognition implementation changes. This would include any change in the entire algorithmic chain: front-end image analysis routines (e.g. face and eye detection); image processing routines (e.g. morphable models to correct for pose), and the feature extraction and back-end matching algorithms.

— **Database effects.** The calibration only applies to images with the properties present in the set.

— **Finite population.** While the curves were estimated using from 400 million comparisons, the population size is still only of size 40000 enrollees, and 10000 impostors.

- **Familial similarities:** The physical structure of the face is genetically linked such that the closely similar facial appearance of identical twins[14] changes only over decades of environmental and developmental influences. Twins have been exploited for criminal purposes [BASIA]. Some face recognition systems appear able to differentiate identical twins by extracting information from the skin texture. Going further, parental and sibling appearance similarities are obvious hazards - the extent to which these could produce anomalously high similarity scores has not been studied here.

- **Ethnic origin:** The calibration applies to the specific population used in the test. This is a mixture of the U. S. persons many of whom have global ethnic ancestry. It is well known that size and appearance are dependent on national and even regional origin. In addition, globalization introduces a time dependency to those categories.

- **Deliberate image manipulation:** It is known [GALBALLY, ADLER] that an image can be automatically adjusted to produce a false match. This has been conceived of to defeat an access control system. While the images produced in an automated hill-climbing scheme can deviate from usual human-form, the extent to which an image can be manipulated to produce a high comparison score while preserving human form is clearly large when the manipulator is a skilled human [MORPH]. In any case, any such activity would be deliberate and fraudulent – the risk of this would be mitigated by the usual evidentiary controls, and could be detected by forensic data analysis [FARID].

INVESTIGATION 12. *Dependence of accuracy on pose*

In 2004, the ISO/IEC 19794-5 standard established limits for deviations from frontal pose (5deg, 5deg, 8deg). These were instituted because pose was known to known to adversely affect facial recognition. Is this still true?

Demand drivers: Previous evaluations have demonstrated that deviations from a fully frontal pose adversely affect recognition accuracy, making individuals more difficult to recognize. The ISO and ANSI/NIST standards limit deviations to avoid this problem, but previous studies have demonstrated that a significant portion of the images in IAFIS have poses deviating more than this requirement.

Prior work: There is an enormous literature on both pose estimation and on improving face recognition under three-axis rotation of the head.

Experimental method: The LEO images were accompanied by subject-specific and image-specific metadata values. In particular each image was accompanied by an estimate of the head pose. Head pose is quantified using the Tait-Bryan angles roll, pitch, and yaw. The estimates were produced by an SDK supplied by an MBE-STILL participant. The SDK was supplied to, and used by, an organization involved in the preparation of the data. It was not used by NIST. The SDK reported an estimate of yaw and roll. All estimates of pitch were zero degrees. The probable reason is the well known lack of a datum for zero pitch in a frontal image.

Yaw measures the degree to which the head is facing left or right (see Figure 18), while roll measures the amount of in-plane rotation of the head (or the camera) about the roll axis.

Figure 18 – Face images from the FERET database demonstrating varying amounts of head yaw.

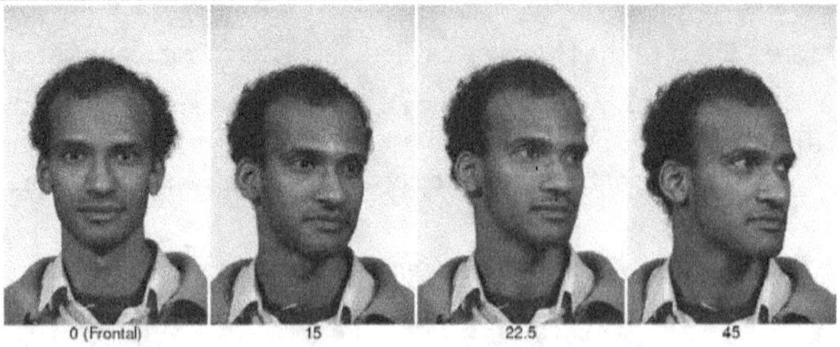

---

[14] And triplets, quadruplets, etc. The natural incidence of n-tuplets is small, and tends to include fraternal rather than identical siblings.

Figure 19 shows the measured distribution of yaw and roll for 590,105 LEO face images. Of these images, 33.6 percent had yaw measurements between -5 and 5 degrees, 86.2 percent had roll measurements between -8 and 8 degrees, and 30.2 percent had yaw and roll measurements within both ranges. Thus, according to these measurements, less than a third of the images fall within the ISO/IEC 19794-5 limitations for deviations from a frontal pose. The black vertical lines highlight the ISO/IEC 19794-5 best practice recommendations for the minimum amount of pose deviation.

Note however that because pitch estimates were unavailable, many images for which yaw assumes a good value will include a significant pitch deviation from what a human observer would consider zero degrees.

Figure 19 – Histograms for yaw and roll angles for LEO images.

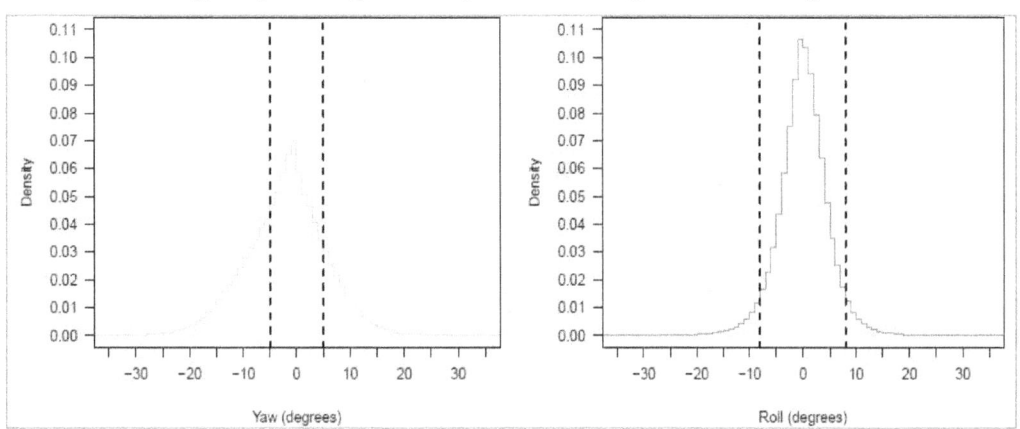

Experimental method: For each SDK we generate templates for all LEO images with one or more mates. We then compute the 1:1 comparison score for each mated pair. This produces 590105 scores. For each pair, we lookup the two yaw-angle estimates.

Results: Figure 20 shows the effect of yaw on the FNMR. The yaw for each comparison was taken as the maximum of the two face images. For most algorithms, error rates are increased when the yaw angle is between 6 and 16 degrees from frontal. Catastrophic failure tends to occur when the yaw angle is greater than 20 degrees. V07 appears the most robust to small-to-moderate deviations in yaw, having the widest U-shaped curve.

Figure 20 – Dependence of accuracy on face yaw angle

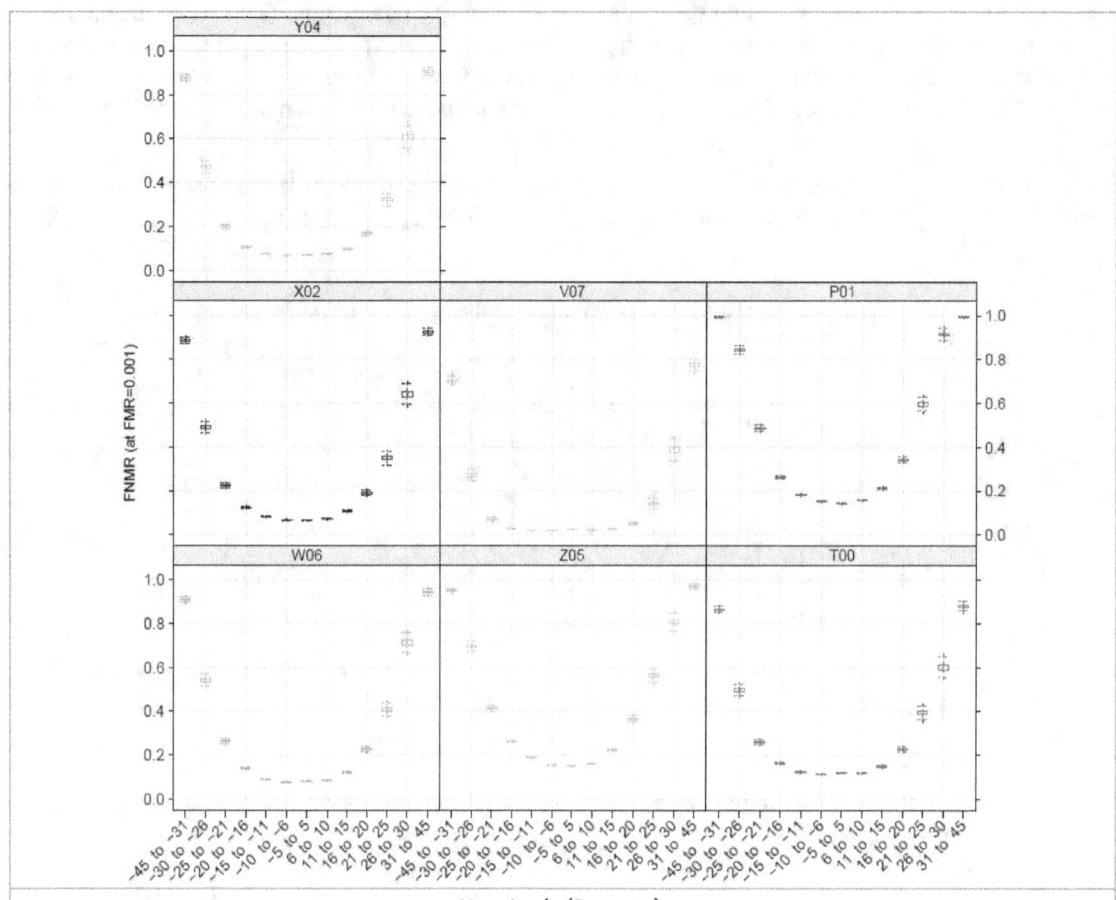

Figure 21 uses *heatmaps* to show the effect of head yaw on the FNMR. Darker colored cells signify higher error rates. This visualization technique has been used before [GROSS] to show increased resistance to pose variation. White colored cells indicate no data was available to compute an FNMR for that cell. The lighter colored cells tend to lie along the main diagonal, indicating error rates are lowest when both face images have similar amounts of yaw. However, unless the yaw angle is similar in both images, catastrophic failure tends to occur if the yaw is greater than 20 degrees in either image.

Figure 21 – Dependence of LEO accuracy on yaw angle of enrollment and verification images

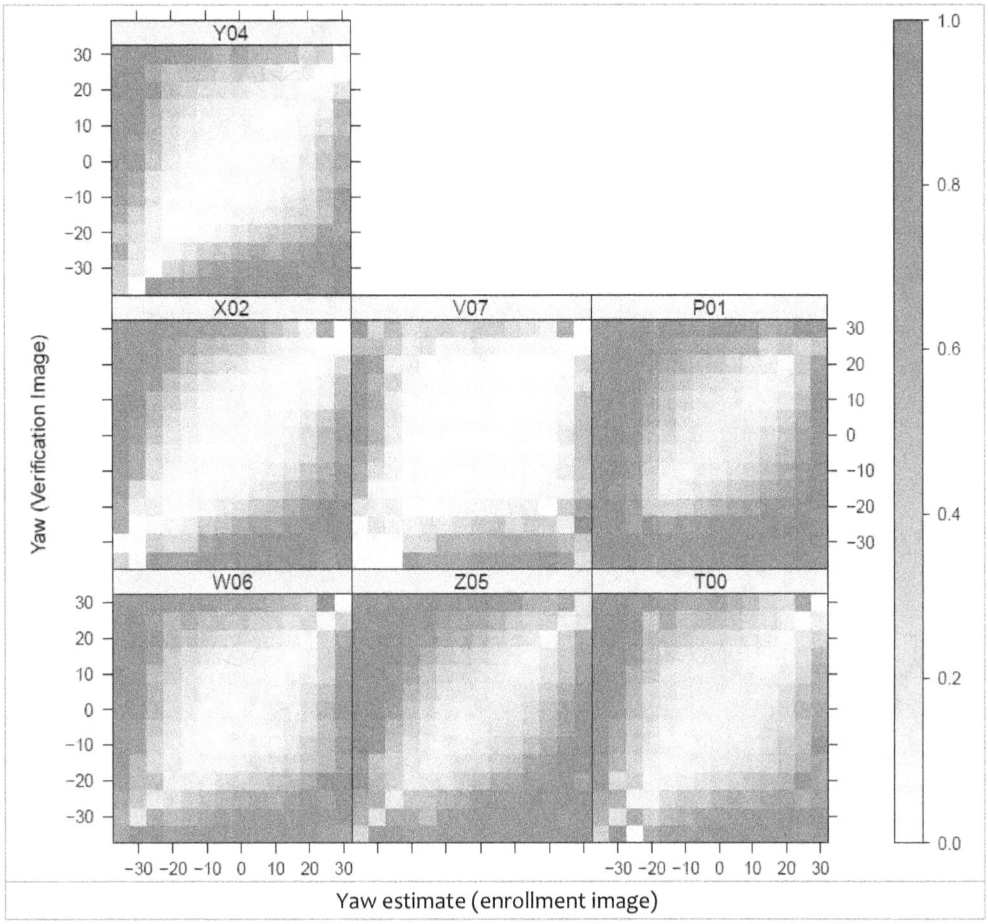

Figure 22 shows the relationship between reported head roll and FNMR. The large increase in error rates as a function of measured roll are mostly due to the roll measurement being accompanied with unmeasured pitch variations (i.e. compound rotations of the head): high amounts of roll also tend face downward. In many cases, high amounts of head roll were reported for images where the eyes were incorrectly located, usually due to considerable amounts of glare from eyeglasses. In these instances, the images suffer from poor sample quality due to a reason other than what was reported. Nevertheless, when a high amount of head roll is reported, it is often indicative of other problems with the image.

Figure 22 – Dependence of LEO accuracy on reported roll angle

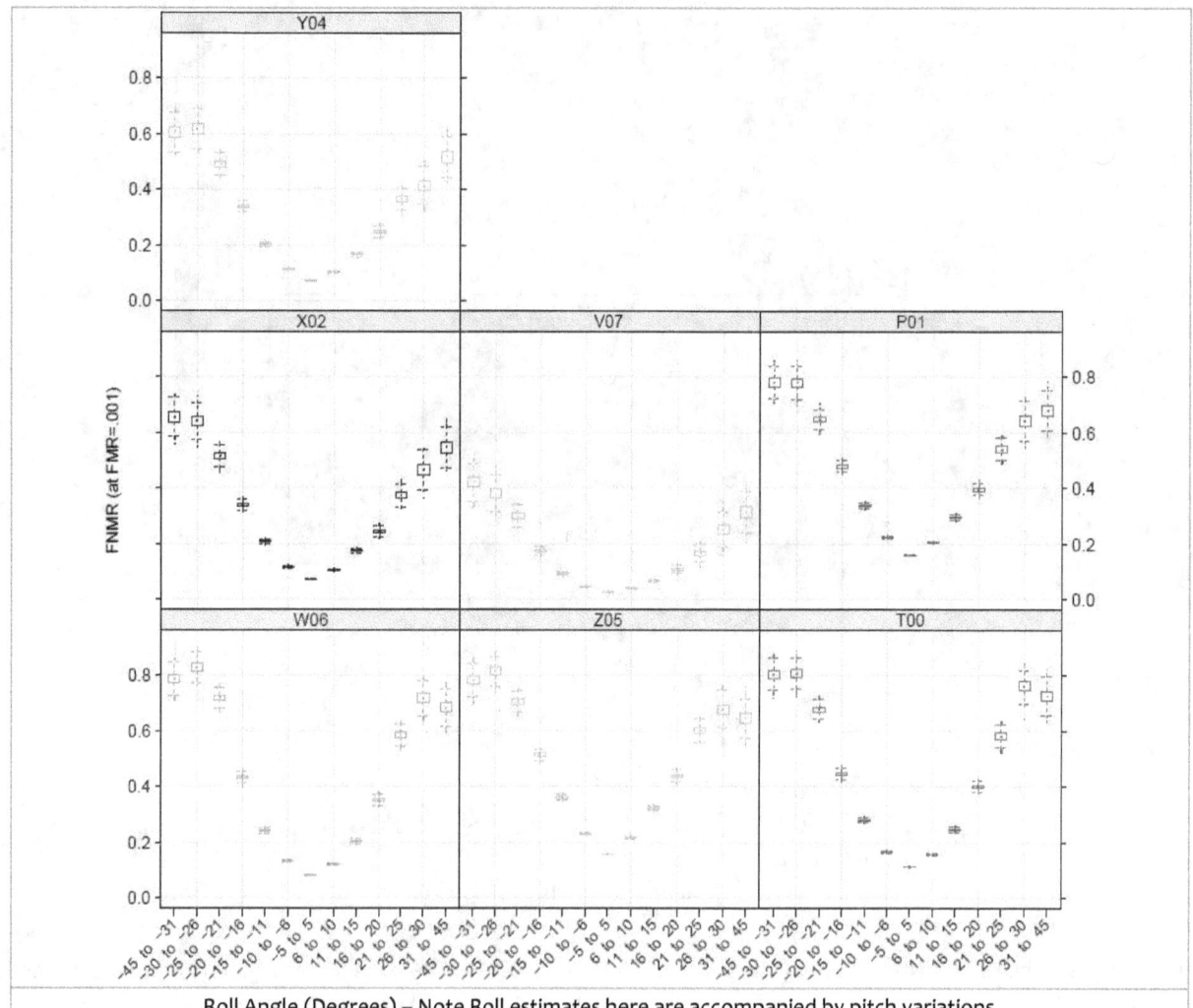

Roll Angle (Degrees) – Note Roll estimates here are accompanied by pitch variations

Conclusions: While the pose problem has received considerable attention in the academic literature, most algorithms tested here will give increased error rates when non-frontal images are acquired and passed on to recognition engines. However, some algorithms are less sensitive to pose angles than others.

INVESTIGATION 13. *Template size*

How big are facial recognition templates? How big are facial images? How do these sizes compare with those of other biometric modalities?

Demand driver: Templates contain the mathematical representation of one or more images of a person. Biometric templates are proprietary, non-standard[15], and their content is protected as a trade-secret.

Template size is clearly influential on storage requirements, both on-disk and in-memory, and on transmission bandwidth requirements. In addition, a large template may be associated with computational complexity and computational expense of the matching algorithm.

Experimental method: The MBE-STILL CONOPS Evaluation Plan and API[16] explicitly supported measurement and reporting of facial recognition template size. When NIST passed K ≥ 1 images to the implementation under test, we

---

[15] Fingerprint minutia templates are the exception in that they are standardized [I378]. While standardized templates can be interoperable (across providers), they offer accuracy below that of proprietary templates [MINEX}.

MBE-STILL REPORT	P = PITTPATT	R = SURREY U.	S = TSINGHUA U.	T = TOSHIBA	U = DALIAN U.	PAGE 48 OF 61
PARTICIPANT KEY	V = NEC	W = L1 IDENTITY	X = COGNITEC	Y = SAGEM	Z = NEUROTECHNOLOGY	

pre-allocated KT bytes, where maximum template size, T, was returned by a function call provided by the implementation under test. The function returned two values, one for maximum enrollment template size, and one for maximum verification or identification template size. For any given input, the actual template size was returned and used to save the template to disk.

Table 22 – On-disk template sizes by SDK and template role

SDK	Class	Enrollment	Verification	SDK	Class	Enrollment	Identification	Notes
P00	A	31349	31349	P03	C	31344	31344	
R00	A	27500	27500					During identification searches the SDK was allowed access to the enrolled templates on hard disk. That is, the API in no way required that all N templates be kept in memory, or to keep whole templates in memory.
R01	A	44200	44200					
S00	A	5520	5520	S06	C		8276	
				S07	C	5520	5520	
T00	A	21760	21760	T02	C	21760	21760	
U00	A	2200	2200					
V00	A	5025	5025	V01	C	5025	5025	The SDK was free to initiate disk access, and to do partial reads of the enrolled data (via, for example, fseek, fread, mmap). This may have been done conditionally, for example reading in proprietary data blocks only during end-stage matching of high scoring candidates.
V04	A	5069	5069	V03	C	5069	5069	
				V06	C	2553	2553	
W01	A	5712	18196	W03	C	5698	18196	
W05	A	5712	18196	W07	C	7775	20273	
W06	A	5698	61830	W08	C	8556	21068	
W10	A	7775		W09	C	8556	21068	
W11	A	6143						
X00	A	4304	4304					The test did not make measurements of peak or mean memory usage during a search.
X01	A	7240	7240	X04	C	7376	7376	
X02	A	7376	7376					
Y00	A	5320	5320	Y03	C		5320	
Y02	A	5752	5752	Y05	C	74056	74056	
				Y06	C	74056	74056	
Z01	A	20488	20488	Z03	C	20488	20488	
Z04	A	24396	24396	Z07	C	33484	33484	
Z05	A	33484	33484					

Results: Table 22 shows template sizes in bytes. These sizes reflect the size of the template in permanent storage (hard disk). More than one provider noted that the matching system does not need to load the entire template into memory for a search. We make the following observations.

— In all cases the size of an enrollment template is independent of the size of the enrolled population. This is not necessarily so because the API supported variable size templates by informing the SDK during initialization of the number of subjects about to be enrolled.

— In all cases except two, the size of the enrollment template size grows linearly with the number of images that went into its creation. The two exceptions are S00 and W03.

— The API supported asymmetric or role-specific templates. This allows a template to be used only for enrollment, or only for recognition but not vice-versa. Many template sizes are independent of role. Notably the enrollment templates for Vendor W are smaller than verification and identification templates. Operationally, a verification template is not stored permanently – it exists only for the duration of a recognition transaction.

— Template sizes are generally larger than those reported for iris recognition [IREX – 10 providers, 19 algorithms].

— Some modest reductions in size are possible via lossless compression (e.g. bzip2).

---

[16] See http://face.nist.gov/mbe/MBE_STILL_Eval_Plan_v1.pdf

As noted previously these template sizes may actually be compound sizes of fast-search and end-stage matcher templates.

Conclusions: Template sizes vary between 2KB and 75KB with strong vendor dependence. Template sizes for verification and identification images sometimes differ from those of enrollment images. Note, however, that several vendors demonstrate an ability to tailor template size quite considerably.

For comparison, templates sizes associated with standardized minutia templates are 0.1 - 0.8 kilobytes [MINEX], with iris recognition 0.5 - 10 kilobytes [IREX], and 1KB to 100KB for proprietary fingerprint templates [PFT].

INVESTIGATION 14. *Template creation time*

How long does it take to extract features from an image and make a template? Does this depend on the width and height of the input image? Does it depend on whether the template is used for enrollment, verification or identification?

Demand driver: Template generation time is often a large component of a 1:1 authentication attempt. For 1:N searches, the fraction will depend on N. Template generation time will be important if an existing image corpus is going to be re-enrolled by a new provider. For example, re-enrollment of a 18M person driving license database takes $1 \times 18 \times 10^{6} / 64 / 3600 = 156$ hours if a one second template generation were sustained on a 32 core blade installation.

Figure 23 – Duration of LEO template generation calls

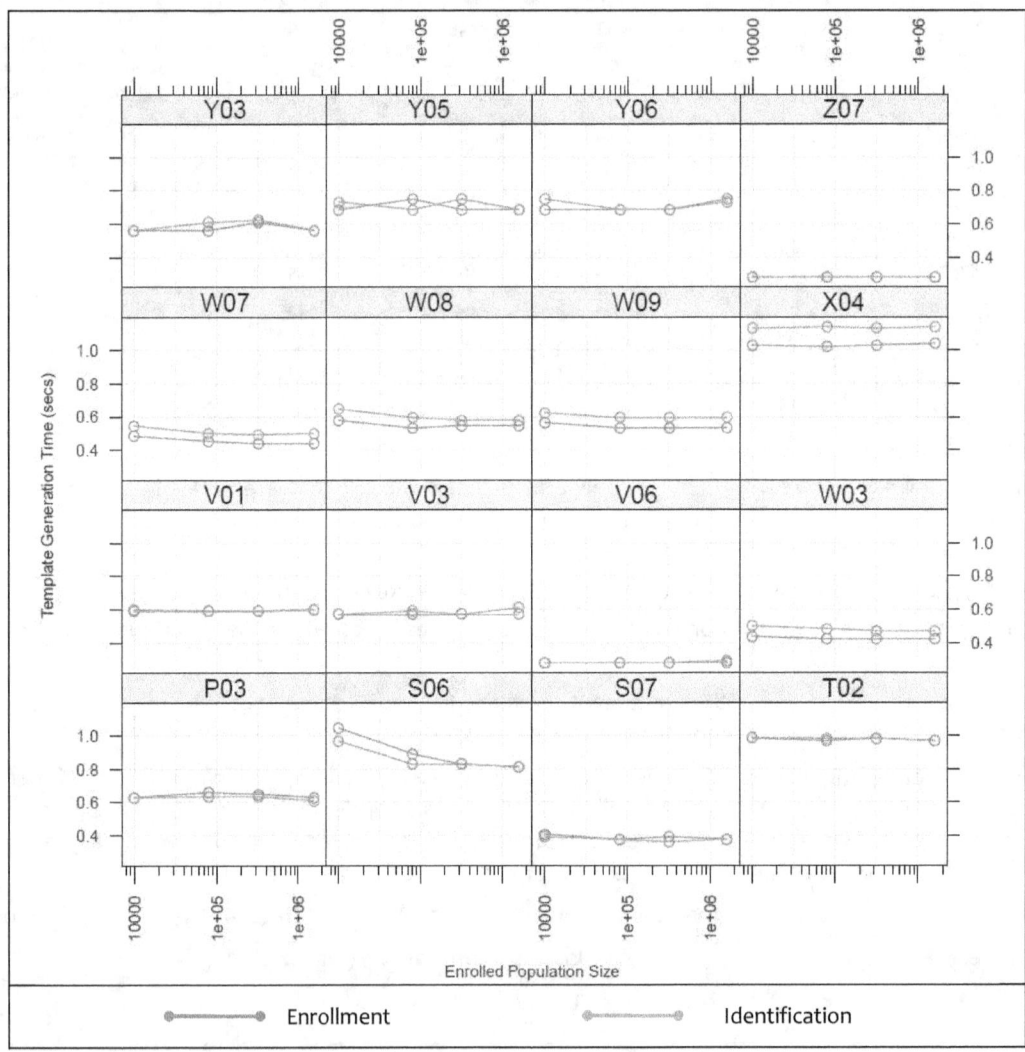

Experimental method: Each template creation function call was wrapped in a timer.

Results: The median duration of the template generation function is reported in Figure 23. The units are seconds. Each panel includes two traces, one for enrollment templates, one for verification templates. One SDK took longer than the 1 second template extraction time limit established in the MBE-STILL API. Note, that algorithm developers did not have access to the target machine, nor to detailed statistics on image dimensions.

Conclusions: Template creation times are independent of the target population size, suggesting that developers did not tailor their algorithmic representation to the size of the identification search.

INVESTIGATION 15. *Link between sex and accuracy*
Are photographs of one sex more readily recognized than those of the other?

Demand driver: Face recognition algorithms should not be too biased in how they treat individuals having certain demographic traits. Preferably, males should not produce score distributions substantially different than females.

Prior work: Previous evaluations have demonstrated that males are easier to recognize than females (FRVT 2002).

Experimental method: MBE-STILL separated 590,105 genuine comparisons from the FBI set into male and female sets. For each algorithm, a distribution of FNMRs (at FMR=0.001) was computed for each sex using 2000 bootstrap iterations. The resulting boxplots show how false non-match error rates differ for the two sexes. The false match rate used in the plots was computed using results from 1:1 comparisons of LEO images.

Certain genuine comparisons were excluded from consideration based on the following criteria:

— If the recorded sex of the individual was not consistent across all captures for that individual.

— If the sex was specified as "Unspecified" or "Unknown".

Results: Table 23 -- LEO Verification accuracy by sexTable 23 shows FNMR for class A verification SDKs broken out by sex.

Table 23 -- LEO Verification accuracy by sex

Class A SDK	FNMR at FMR = 0.001		Notes
	Male	Female	
W06	0.111	0.113	The standard
Z05	0.193	0.200	errors for these
T00	0.145	0.137	measurements
X02	0.095	0.109	are about 0.001
V07	0.039	0.042	for females and
P01	0.187	0.214	0.0004 for
Y04	0.094	0.111	males.

Conclusions: Males generate fewer false non-matches than females for five of the six algorithms, although the disparity is small in every case. Since the FRVT 2002 Evaluation, the link between sex and genuine scores appears to have diminished. However, this may arise because different datasets with different demographic properties were used (LEO vs. DOS/HCINT). The relationship between sex and impostor scores was not investigated here.

INVESTIGATION 16. *Link between subject age and accuracy*
Are older subjects easier or more difficult to recognize?

Demand driver: Face recognition algorithms should not be too biased in how they treat individuals having certain demographic traits. In addition, investigating a possible age effect can potentially identify aspects of automated face recognition that require improvement.

Prior work: Previous evaluations have demonstrated that older individuals are easier to recognize than younger ones [FRVT 2002].

Experimental method: MBE-STILL binned 590,105 genuine comparisons from the FBI set into 5-year age groups. For each algorithm, and within each age group, a distribution of FNMRs (at FMR=0.001) was computed using 2000 bootstrap iterations. The resulting plots show how false non-match error rates differ for the different age groups. Age was assigned to genuine comparisons based on the time elapsed between the individual's birth date, and the date at which the first (i.e. oldest) image was captured. The false match rate used in the plots was computed using results from 1:1 comparisons of LEO images.

Results: While an age effect is clearly displayed for most algorithms, the precise behavior differs for each algorithm. The most defined trend is with V07, where an older individual ($\geq$ 60 years old) is several times more likely to be missed than a younger person (< 30 years old). Most of the other trends are not as severe. Nor are they monotonic, since a jump in the FNMR is often present around the 30-34 age group. While an obvious concern is that the age effect may be confounded with the time elapsed between photographs, this doesn't seem likely for the V07 SDK which shows resistance to elapsed time (see Figure 25).

Figure 24 – LEO Verification accuracy by age of subject at most recent capture

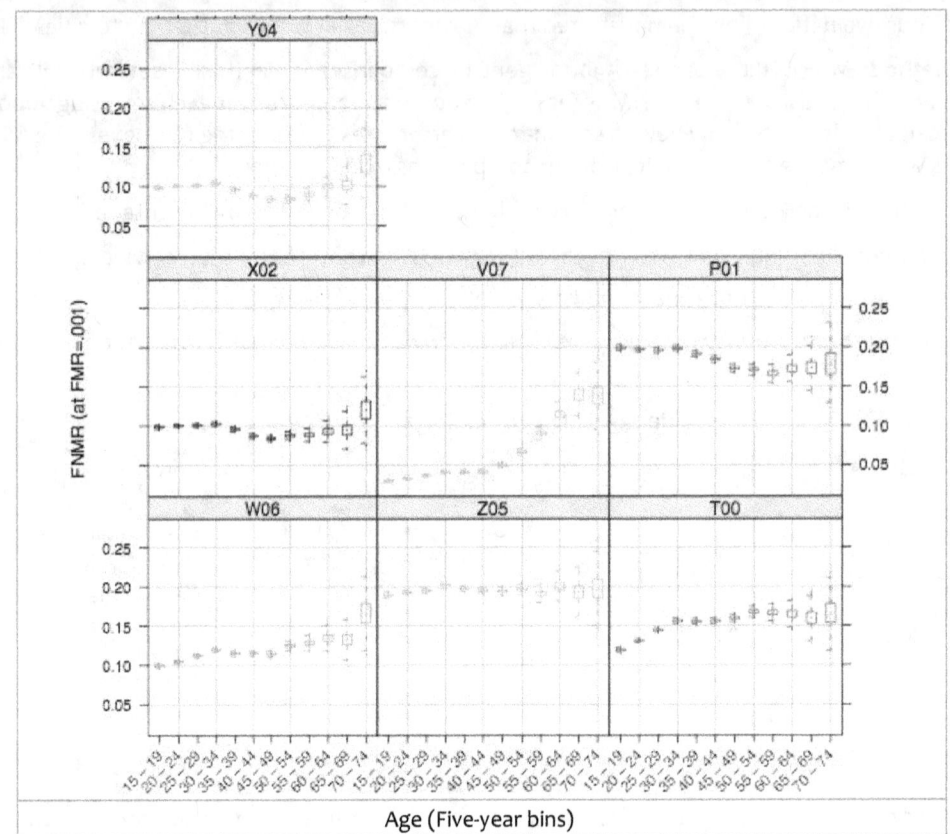

Conclusions: The effect of subject age depends on which algorithm is used. In most cases the effect is small, and smaller than that reported previously [FRVT2002]. The one exception, for one of the more accurate implementations, is an increase in FNMR of more than a factor of five. While, this result may prompt consideration by the developer, the effect is again subject to confounding factors in the data.

INVESTIGATION 17. *Face ageing*

Faces change over time. While no large and long-term face image collection exists, has the resistance of face recognition algorithms to age-related changes improved since it was reported in FRVT 2002?

Demand driver: False rejection errors will increase if the facial appearance changes significantly over time. The causes are not limited to just ageing. Other drivers include weight change, sun exposure, drug use, facial hair growth or removal, and posture changes related to skeletal changes (scoliosis). While research has been conducted to model ageing [RAMANATHAN] and to build age-independent representations [PARK], the primary means to mitigate time-related changes is to re-enroll cooperative users, when it is practical and cost-effective.

Prior work: Several projects have specifically set out to collect facial images for the purposes of supporting research and development in this area (See particularly the large datasets collected under the MORPH project (Craniofacial Longitudinal Morphological Face Database), www.faceaginggroup.com, and the FG-NET work www.fgnet.rsunit.com. NIST's primary approach has been to leverage operational data for which date-of-capture metadata is available.

Experimental method: A key assumption of the analysis is that while any given pair of face images might yield a false rejection due to non-age related reasons (typically pose, illumination or expression effects), the average over a large number of facial comparisons will quantify age-related effects. This also assumes that there is no systematic change in the imaging collection practice and design over the interval.

Results: Figure 25 shows an increase in FNMR occurs as the time between captures increases, although some algorithms appear more robust to aging than others. The horizontal axis stretches from 0 months to 95 months (~8 years). Based upon a visual inspection, the increased FNMR for the 0-5 month bin is the result of same-day profile images being mislabeled as frontal. For most of the algorithms, the FNMR increases as the time between captures extends from 6-11 months to 30-35 months. Beyond that, many of the algorithms display a counter-intuitive decrease in the FNMR as the time between captures extends from 30-35 months to about 66-71 months. This may be the result of hidden factors (i.e. there may be some property of the face images within this range that makes them easier to recognize that is not directly related to aging of the face).

Figure 25 – LEO Verification accuracy by time elapsed between photographs

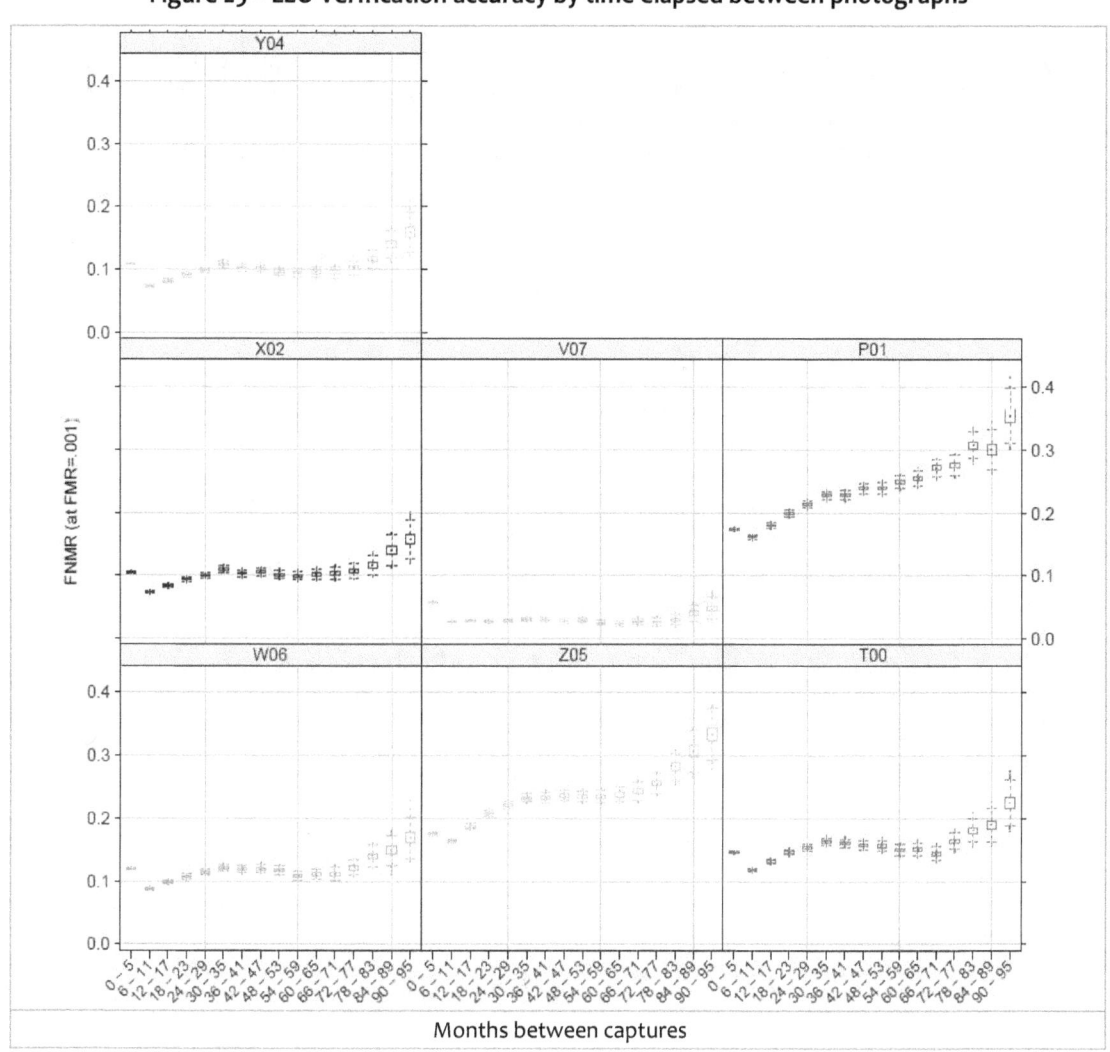

MBE-STILL REPORT PARTICIPANT KEY	P = PITTPATT	R = SURREY U.	S = TSINGHUA U.	T = TOSHIBA	U = DALIAN U.	PAGE 53 OF 61
	V = NEC	W = L1 IDENTITY	X = COGNITEC	Y = SAGEM	Z = NEUROTECHNOLOGY	

Conclusions: For most verification algorithms, false non-match rates increase by roughly a factor of two over the eight year interval represented in the LEO dataset. Any proposal to extend re-enrollment intervals for face-based verification systems is not supported by the results here. However, one algorithm does exhibit greater resistance to elapsed time. This is unlikely to be a random effect, but given the presence of confounding factors, such as subject age, a more detailed statistical analysis is warranted.

INVESTIGATION 18. *Is subject weight influential?*
Are photographs of lighter subjects more readily recognized than those of heavy subjects?

Demand driver: A person's weight is reflected in his physical appearance. Knowing how weight affects recognition accuracy may provide information that could be exploited to improve the accuracy of recognition systems.

Prior work: The author is not aware of any.

Experimental method: MBE-STILL binned 590,105 genuine comparisons from the FBI set into 10 kg weight increments. For each algorithm, and within each weight increment, a distribution of FNMRs (at FMR=.001) was computed using 2000 bootstrap iterations. Comparisons were further separated into male and female groups since females tend to weigh less, which could introduce a bias if recognition accuracy differs for the different sexes. The resulting plot shows how the false non-match rate changes across weight increments. Weight was assigned to genuine comparisons based on the average of the weights reported for the two captures. The false match rate was computed using results from study 3.

Results: Figure 26 shows, for class A verification SDKs, the dependence of FNMR on subject weight, broken out by subject sex. The threshold is set to produce FMR = 0.001. In all cases, heavier set individuals appear easier to recognize, as most of the figures display a downward trend from left to right. It is possible that a higher amount of body fat introduces additional distinctive features in the face (e.g. folds under the chin). The trend may also be the result of one or more hidden factors, although separating comparisons into male and female sets precludes sex as such a factor. A follow-up investigation (not shown) revealed that the change in weight between captures of an individual had only a very small effect on recognition accuracy, much less than the individual's average weight.

Figure 26 – LEO Verification accuracy by subject weight

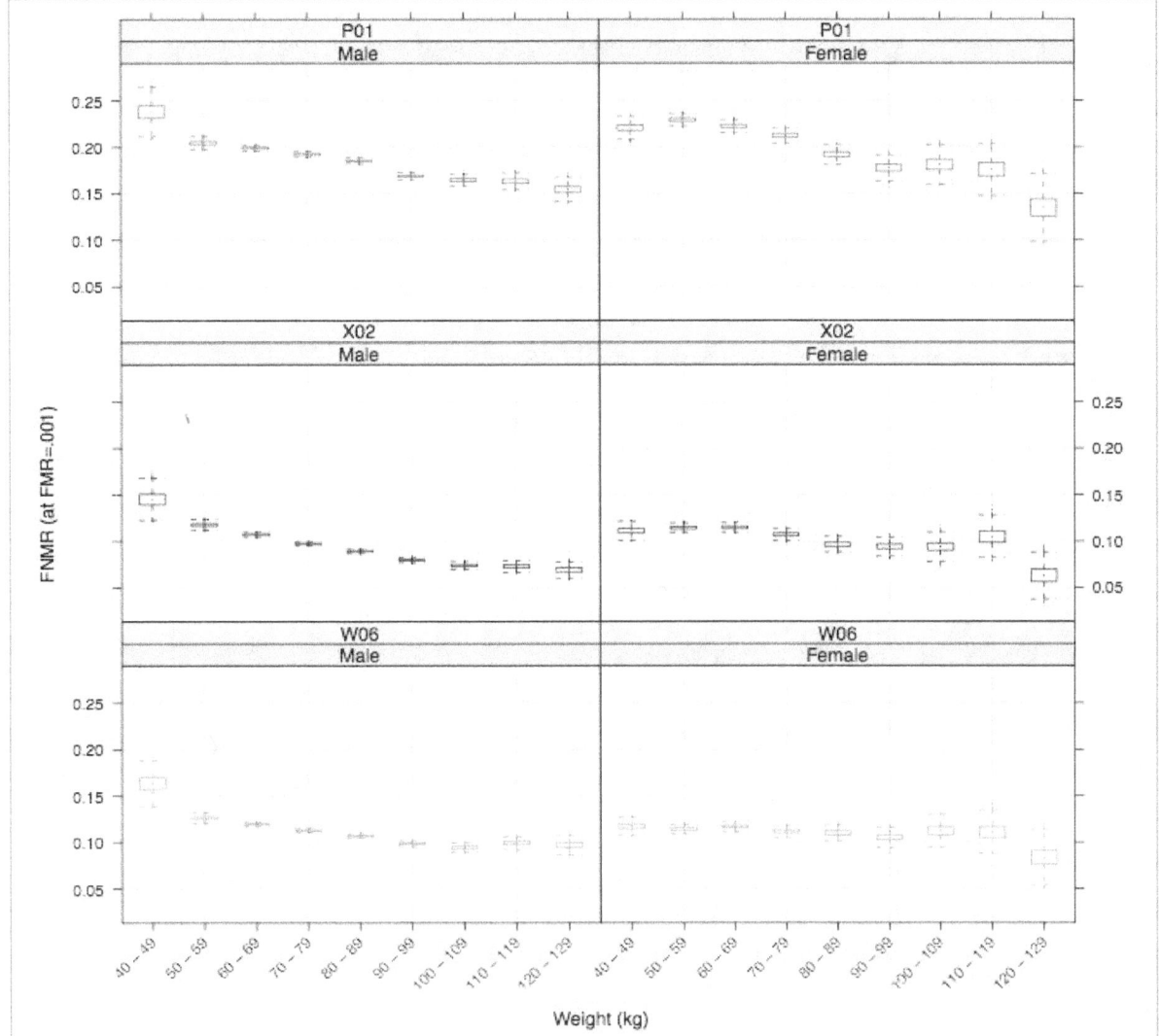

Conclusion: While an accuracy trend is clearly evident for both males and females, the result is largely unimportant operationally because weight is not usually a controllable factor, and because the highest error rates are associated with relatively rare individuals with weight below 50 kilograms. The current analysis does not reveal whether this result is confounded with the presence of minors in the dataset. Further statistical analysis is warranted.

INVESTIGATION 19. *Link Between race and accuracy*
How does race affect the ease of recognition?

Demand driver: Face recognition algorithms should not be too biased in how they treat individuals having certain demographic traits. In addition, investigating a possible race effect can potentially identify aspects of automated face recognition that could be improved.

Prior work: The link between race and automated face recognition has been analyzed in several prior studies [QUINN, FRVT 2002].

Experimental method: 590,105 genuine comparisons from the FBI set were separated by race. For each algorithm, and for each race, a distribution of FNMRs (at FMR=0.001) was computed using 2000 bootstrap iterations. The resulting plot shows how the false non-match rate differs for different races. A given genuine comparison was only retained if the recorded race was consistent across all image captures for the given individual. The false match rate was computed using results from study 3.

Results: Figure 27 shows, for class A verification SDKs, the dependence of FNMR on subject weight, broken out by subject ethnicity code. The threshold is set to produce FMR = 0.001.

Conclusions: A race effect clearly exists for each of the algorithms. Blacks are easier to recognize than whites for 5 of the 6 algorithms. American Indians and Asians were clearly easier to recognize for 3 of the algorithms (P01, Z05, and T00), while for V07 American Indians and Asians appeared more difficult to recognize. Disparities in the performance of face recognition algorithms across races has been documented previously [PHILLIPS], and in many cases may simply be due to differing training procedures that are aimed at optimizing performance for an expected demographic.

Figure 27 – LEO Verification accuracy by ethnic category

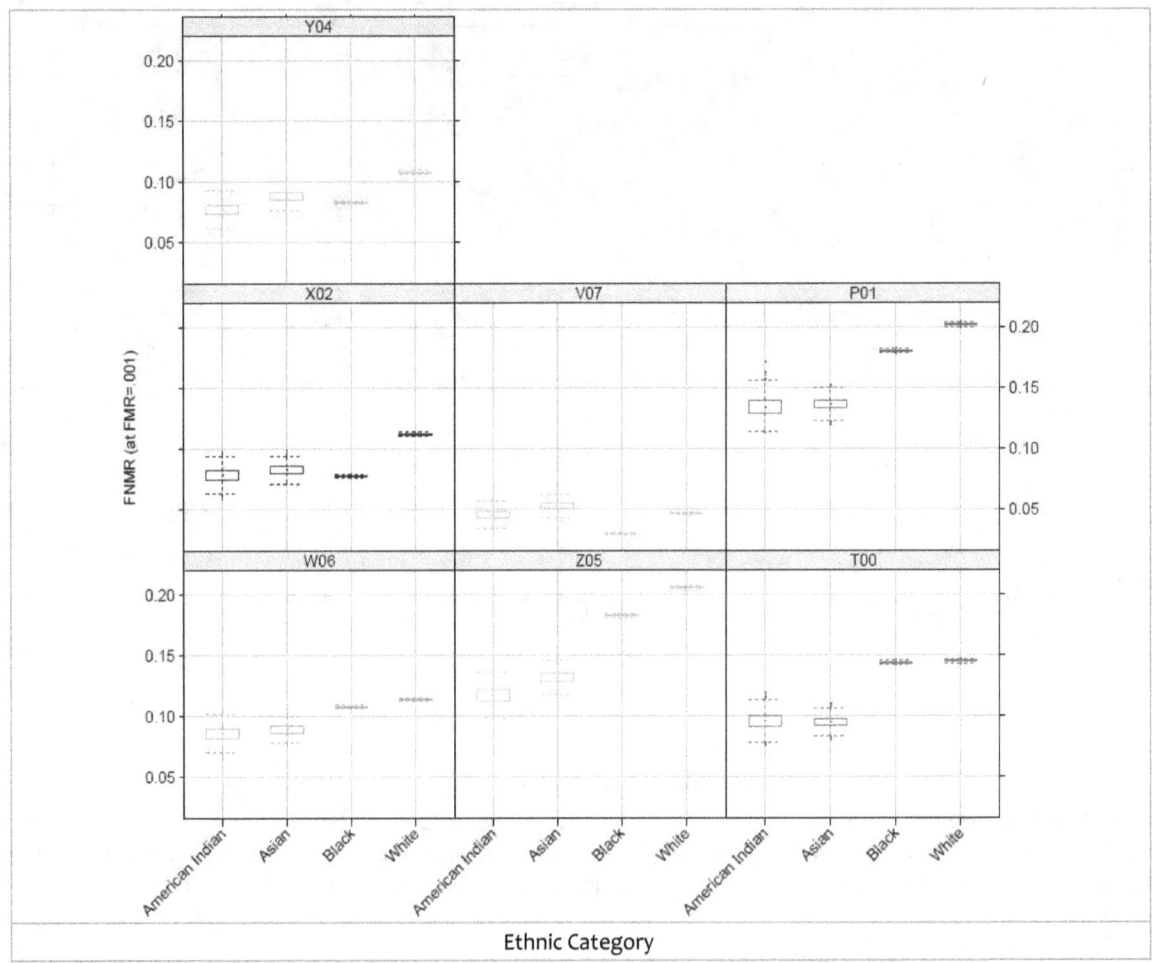

INVESTIGATION 20. *Value of biographic data*

If a facial recognition implementation is provided with subject-specific biographic metadata, can accuracy be improved?

Demand driver: In many large-scale identity management applications, biometric data is collected with accompanying metadata such as sex, weight, height or ethnicity. Some of these pieces of information meet certain of the qualifications for being biometric data in their own right but are, by themselves, obviously of limited value for identification.

Such data is often entered by a human operator and is subject to error. This can arise due to clerical and typographic errors, and systemic effects (e.g. non-compliance to the ISO 8601 standard for dates. Unreliable data can undermine identity management. Indeed biometrics is often advanced as an answer to clerical errors. An additional operational concern is that in some applications such data can be clearly incorrect or spoofed. That said, identity management applications such as PIV routinely protect the integrity of biographical information by computing the digital signature over biometric records (i.e. data + header, for example CBEFF [PIV]). In any case, the MBE-STILL was initiated to include a study of whether biometric recognition process could be augmented by the use of metadata such as sex and age.

Prior work: This issue has been studied in the academic literature [FIERREZ, ROSS].

Experimental method: The MBE-STILL API supported the provision of the biographical metadata for an image to the SDK[17]. The list of variables is: sex, age, height, weight, ethnicity, date of birth, and date of photograph. These are supplied to the face image data-structure that is input to the template generator. The experiment proceeds by running an identical face recognition trial with and without metadata, and comparing the measured accuracy.

NIST only provided the developers with metadata information in late April 2010 just weeks before the closure of the submission window and the scheduled issuance of the first report. The data provided was for the MEDS dataset. This gave algorithm providers a very short period for its analysis and exploitation. In late May 2010, the authors asked whether vendors attempted to use metadata. None made any claim that this data was valuable.

Conclusions: We found no evidence that algorithms exploit date information. This is likely a consequence that algorithm developers have a) never been contracted or challenged to affirmatively incorporate date information, and b) have insufficient data with which to calibrate their reliance on the metadata. This negative result may be valuable to others' considering this issue.

Figure 28 – Progression of face recognition accuracy measurements

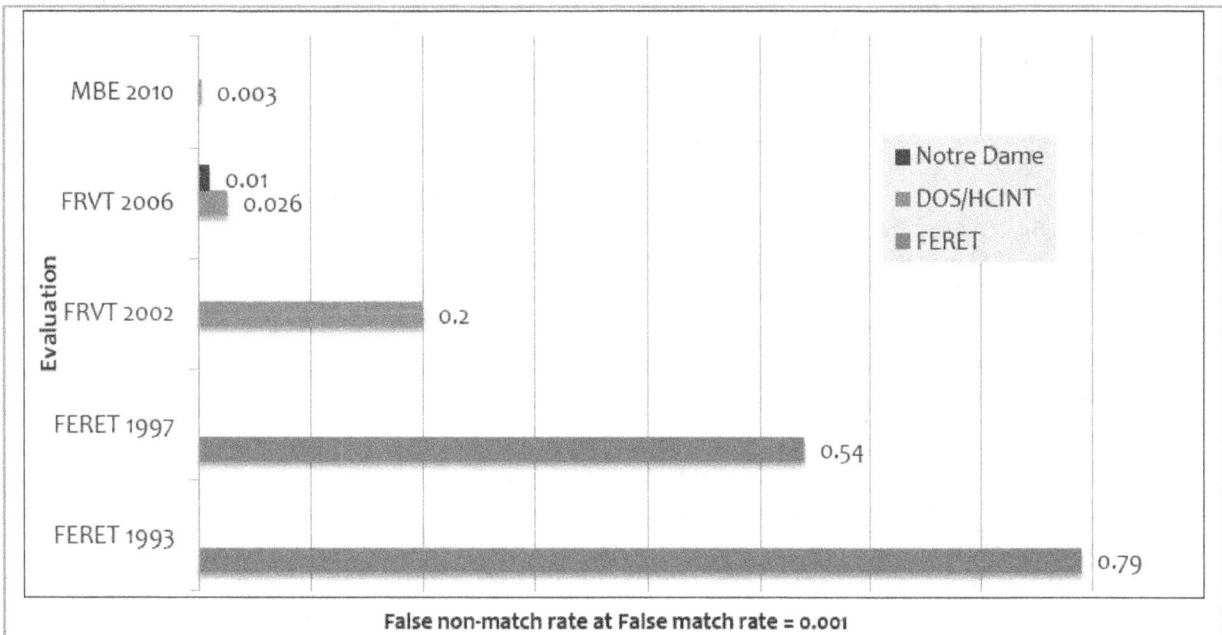

The reduction in error rate for state-of-the-art face recognition algorithms as documented through the FERET, the FRVT 2002, the FRVT 2006, and the MBE 2010 Still Face evaluations. Performance is broken out by the FERET, DOS/HCINT, and the Notre Dame FRVT 2006 data sets.

---

[17] These were sex, ethnicity, date of birth, date of capture, height and weight. See Table 9 of the NIST Concept, API and Evaluation plan for the data structures and units.

7.   Progress in face recognition

The face recognition community has benefited from a series of U.S. Government funded technology development efforts and evaluation cycles, beginning with the FERET program in September 1993. The evaluations have documented roughly three orders-of-magnitude improvement in performance from the start of the FERET program through the MBE 2010 Still Face.

Figure 28 quantifies this improvement at five key milestones. For each milestone, verification performance is report. Performance report is the false non-match rate (FNMR) at a false match rate (FMR) of 0.001 (1 in 1000) and is given for a representative state-of-the-art algorithm. The 1993 milestone is a retrospective implementation of Turk and Pentland's eigenface algorithm [TURK], which was partially automatic (it required that eye coordinates be provided). Performance is reported on the eigenface implementation of Moon and Phillips [MOON] with the FERET Sept96 protocol [FERET], in which images of a subject were taken on different days (dup I probe set). The 1997 milestone is for the Sept97 FERET evaluation, which was conducted at the conclusion of the FERET program. Performance is quoted on the U. of Southern California's fully automatic submission to the final FERET evaluation [WISKOTT, OKADA]. The 1993 and 1997 results are on the same test dataset and show improvement in algorithm technology under the FERET program. Technology improved from partially automatic to fully automatic algorithms, while error rate declined by approximately a third.

The 2002 benchmark is from the FRVT 2002 [FRVT2002]. In the FRVT 2002 verification performance was reported for the Cognitec, Eyematic, and Identix submissions on the DOS/HCINT dataset. Because both the FERET and DOS/HCINT datasets are low-resolution and have similar performance on the baseline algorithm (see Table V in Phillips et. al [FRVT2006]), one can make the case that they are comparable and a significant portion of the decrease error rate was due to algorithm improvement.

The 2006 benchmark is from the FRVT 2006 [FRVT2006]. In Figure 28, performance is reported for both the Notre Dame high-resolution controlled-illumination still images and the DOS/HCINT dataset. The Notre Dame data set was collected under laboratory conditions. On the Notre Dame data set, the submission from Neven Vision achieved a FNMR of 0.008 at a FMR of 0.001. On the DOS/HCINT data set, Toshiba achieved a FNMR of 0.026 at a FMR of 0.001.

The 2010 benchmark is from the DOS/HCINT data set in Investigation 7. In Investigation 7, a FNMR of 0.003 at a FMR of 0.001 was achieved for the NEC submission. This performance shows a decrease in the FMNR at a FMR = 0.001 from 0.79 in 1993 to 0.003 in 2010. The 1993 benchmark is for a partial automatic algorithm on the FERET data set, which was a laboratory-collected data set. The 2010 benchmark was on an operational data set. The decrease the error rate is roughly three orders-of-magnitude while moving from performance of a partially automatic algorithm on laboratory data set to a fully automatic commercial system on operational data.

8. References

8.1. Publications and Reports

ADLER	A. Adler, *Images can be regenerated from quantized biometric match score data*, in Canadian Conference on Electrical and Computer Engineering, pages 469–472, May 2004. A. Adler, *Vulnerabilities in biometric encryption systems*, in International Conference on Audio and Video based Biometric Person Authentication, pages 1100–1109, July 2005.
BLUMENSTEIN	*Random parameter stochastic process models of criminal careers.* In Blumstein, Cohen, Roth & Visher (Eds.), Criminal Careers and Career Criminals, Washington, D.C.: National Academy of Sciences Press, 1986.
BOLLE	Ruud Bolle, Jonathon Connell, Sharanthchandra Pankanti, Nalini Ratha, *Andrew Senior, Guide to Biometrics Springer,* November, 2003.
CHUTORIAN	E. Murphy-Chutorian and M. Trivedi, *Head Pose Estimation in Computer Vision: A Survey in* IEEE Trans. on Pattern Analysis and Machine Intelligence (PAMI), April 2009, vol. 31, no. 4.
DODDINGTON	G. Doddington, W. Liggett, A. Martin, M. Przybocki, and D. Reynolds, *Sheep, Goats, Lambs and Woves: An Analysis of Individual Differences in Speaker Recognition Performance*, in the International Conference on Spoken Language Processing (ICSLP), Sydney, 1998.
FARID	H. Farid, *Exposing Digital Forgeries from JPEG Ghosts*, in IEEE Transactions on Information Forensics and Security, Vol. 1, No 4. Pp 154-160, 2009. See also H. Farid, *A Survey of Image Forgery Detection*, IEEE Signal Processing Magazine, No. 26, Vol. 2. 2009.
FERET	P. J. Phillips, H. Moon, S. A. Rizvi, and P. J. Rauss, *The FERET evaluation methodology for face-recognition algorithms*, IEEE Trans. Pattern Analysis and Machine Intelligence, Vol. 22, 1090-1104, 2000.
FIERREZ	J. Fierrez-Aguilar et al. *Exploiting general knowledge in user-dependent fusion strategies for multimodal biometric verification.* In Proc IEEE International Conference on Acoustics, Speech, and Signal Processing (ICASSP), 2004.
FONDEUR	Jean-Christophe Fondeur, *Biometric Testing and Performance Extrapolation*, in Proc. International Biometric Performance Conference (IBPC), March 4, 2010. Linked from: http://biometrics.nist.gov/ibpc2010/presentations.html
FRVT 2002	P. Jonathon Phillips, Patrick Grother, Ross J. Micheals, Duane M. Blackburn, Elham Tabassi, Mike Bone, *Face Recognition Vendor Test 2002: Evaluation Report*, NIST Interagency Report 6965.
FRVT 2004	Patrick Grother and George W. Quinn, *Unpublished study for DHS.* May 2004.
FRVT 2002b	Patrick Grother, *Face Recognition Vendor Test 2002: Supplemental Report*, NIST Interagency Report 7083,
FRVT 2006	P. J. Phillips, W. T. Scruggs, A. J. O'Toole, P. J. Flynn, K. W. Bowyer, C. L. Schott, M. Sharpe, "FRVT 2006 and ICE 2006 Large Scale Results," IEEE Trans. Pattern Analysis and Machine Intelligence, Vol 32, pp 831—846, 2010. P. Jonathon Phillips, W. Todd Scruggs, Alice J. O'Toole, Patrick J. Flynn, Kevin W. Bowyer, Cathy L. Schott, and Matthew Sharpe. *FRVT 2006 and ICE 2006 Large-Scale Results.* NISTIR 7408, March 2007.
GALBALLY	J. Galbally, C. McCool, J. Fierrez, S. Marcel, and J. Ortega-Garcia, *On the vulnerability of face verification systems to hill-climbing attacks*, Pattern Recognition, Volume 43 , Issue 3, March 2010, pp. 1027-1038.
GROSS	Ralph Gross, Simon Baker, Iain Matthews, and Takeo Kanade, *Face Recognition Across Pose and Illumination*, Chap 9 in Handbook of Face Recognition, Li et al eds. Springer, 2005.
GROTHER	Patrick Grother, P. Jonathon Phillips, Models of Large Population Performance, Proc. IEEE Conference on Computer Vision and Pattern Recognition (CVPR), pp. 68-75, Vol 2. June 2004.
GREATHOUSE	DHS Latent Print Activities, D. Greathouse, in Proceedings of the Latent Fingerprint Testing Workshop, NIST, March 19-20, 2009. http://fingerprint.nist.gov/latent/workshop09/presentations.htm
HUBE	Jens Peter Hube, *Using Biometric Verification to Estimate Identification Performance*, In Proc. Biometrics Symposium 2006 (BSYM), http://www.biometrics.org/bc2006/program.htm

IREX	Patrick Grother, Elham Tabassi, George W. Quinn and Wayne Salamon, *Performance and Interoperability of Iris Images Performance of Iris Recognition Algorithms on Standard Images*. NIST Interagency Report 7629, October 30, 2009. Linked from http://iris.nist.gov/irex
JAROSZ	Herve Jarosz and Jean-Christophe Fondeur, *Large Scale Identification System Design*, Chap 9 in Biometric Systems Wayman et al. eds. Springer 2005.
MARTIN	Brian Martin, *Biometric Identification: Metrics & Models*, in Proc. International Biometric Performance Conference (IBPC), March 4, 2010. Linked from: http://biometrics.nist.gov/ibpc2010/presentations.html
MEAGHER	Stephen B. Meagher, *Defining AFIS Latent Print "Lights-Out"*, in Proc. Eval. of Latent Fingerprint Technologies Workshop, NIST, March 19-20, 2009. http://fingerprint.nist.gov/latent/workshop09/presentations.htm
MIN	J Min, K W Bowyer, P Flynn, *Using multiple gallery and probe images per person to improve performance of face recognition*, Notre Dame Computer Science and Engineering Technical Report (2003).
MINEX	P. Grother et al., *Performance and Interoperability of the INCITS 378 Template*, NIST IR 7296 http://fingerprint.nist.gov/minex04/minex_report.pdf
NUPPENEY	EasyPASS – Evaluation of face recognition performance in an operational automated border control system, in Proc. International Biometric Performance Conference (IBPC), March 2, 2010. Linked from http://biometrics.nist.gov/ibpc2010/presentations.html
MOC	P. Grother and W. Salamon, *MINEX II - An Assessment of ISO/IEC 7816 Card-Based Match-on-Card Capabilities* http://fingerprint.nist.gov/minex/minexII/NIST_MOC_ISO_CC_interop_test_plan_1102.pdf
NANDAKUMAR	Karthik Nandakumar, Arun Ross and Anil K. Jain, *Biometric Fusion: Does Modeling Correlation Really Matter?* In Proc. Third IEEE International Conference on Biometrics: Theory, Applications and Systems – BTAS 2009.
OKADA	K. Okada, J. Steffens, T. Maurer, H. Hong, E. Elagin, H. Neven, and C. von der Malsburg, *The Bochum/USC face recognition system*, in Face Recognition: From Theory to Applications, H. Wechsler, P. J. Phillips, V. Bruce, F. Fogelman Soulie , and T. S. Huang, Eds. Berlin: Springer-Verlag, 1998, pp. 186-205.
PARK	Unsang Park, Yiying Tong, Anil K. Jain, *Age-Invariant Face Recognition*, IEEE Transactions on Pattern Analysis and Machine Intelligence, pp. 947-954, May, 2010
PHILLIPS	J. Phillips, F. Jiang, A. Narvekar, J. Ayyad, and A. O'Toole, *An Other Race Effect for Face Recognition Algorithms*. NIST IR 7666. http://face.nist.gov/NISTIR-7666_Algorithm_Other_Race_Effect.pdf.
PINELLAS	Jim Main and Scott McCallum, *Face Recognition; The Pinellas County Sherriff's Office Experience*, Proc. Biometrics Consortium, 2003. http://biometrics.org/bc2003/program.htm Case Study, Pinellas Country Sherriff's Office (PCSO) Improves Law Enforcement, L1 ID. http://www.l1id.com/files/488-SCD_Pinellas_Case_study_FINAL.pdf
QUINN	G. W. Quinn, P. Grother, *False Matches and Non-independence of Face Recognition Scores*, in the 2nd international Conference on Biometrics: Theory, Applications and Systems (BTAS) 2008.
RAMANATHAN	Narayanan Ramanathan and Rama Chellappa, Modeling Age Progression in Young Faces, Proc. IEEE Conference on Computer Vision and Pattern Recognition (CVPR), pp. 387-394, Vol 1. June 2006.
ROSS	Arun Ross and Norman Poh, *Multibiometric Systems: Overview, Case Studies and Open Issues*, in Handbook of Remote Biometricsfor Surveillance and Security, Tistarelli, Li, Chellappa (Eds.), Springer, 2009.
SHAKNAROVICH	Gregory Shakhnarovich, John W. Fisher, and Trevor Darrell, Face recognition from long-term observations, Proceedings of the 7th European Conference on Computer Vision (ECCV), Part III, pp. 851 - 868, 2002. AI Laboratory, MIT.
SHERRAH	Jamie Sherrah, *False Alarm Rate: a Critical Performance Measure for Face Recognition* in Proc. IEEE Conf on Automatic Face and Gesture Recognition, (FG'04), 2004. Seoul, Korea
TURK	M. Turk and A. Pentland, *Eigenfaces for recognition*,' J. Cognitive Neuroscience, Vol. 3, No. 1, pp. 71-86, 1991
WAGGETT	Peter Waggett, Henry Bloomfield, Bill Perry John Marc Gibbon Jeremy Monroe, Jean-Christophe Fondeur, Reducing Risk Through Large Scale Testing. In Proc. International Biometric Performance Conference (IBPC), March 2, 2010. Linked from http://biometrics.nist.gov/ibpc2010/presentations.html

WEIN	Wein, L. and Baveja, M., "Using fingerprint image quality to improve the identification performance of the U.S. Visitor and Immigrant Status Indicator Technology Program," Proc. National Acad. Sci., v102, pp. 7772-7775, 2005.
WISKOTT	L. Wiskott, J.-M. Fellous, N. Kruger, and C. von der Malsburg, ``Face recognition by elastic bunch graph matching,'' IEEE Trans. Pattern Analysis and Machine Intelligence, Vol.~17, pp. 775-779, 1997.

8.2.   Standards

AN27	NIST Special Publication 500-271: American National Standard for Information Systems — *Data Format for the Interchange of Fingerprint, Facial, & Other Biometric Information – Part 1.* (ANSI/NIST ITL 1-2007). Approved April 20, 2007.
ISO STD05	ISO/IEC 19794-5:2005 — *Information technology — Biometric data interchange formats — Part 5: Face image data.* The standard was published in 2005, and can be purchased from ANSI at http://webstore.ansi.org/ Multipart standard of "Biometric data interchange formats". This standard was published in 2005. It was amended twice to include guidance to photographers, and then to include 3D information. Two corrigenda were published. All these changes and new material is currently being incorporated in revision of the standard. Publication is likely in early 2011. The documentary history is as follows. 1. ISO/IEC 19794-5: Information technology — Biometric data interchange formats — Part 5:Face image data. First edition: 2005-06-15. 2. International Standard ISO/IEC 19794-5:2005 Technical Corrigendum 1: Published 2008-07-01 3. International Standard ISO/IEC 19794-5:2005 Technical Corrigendum 2: Published 2008-07-01 4. Information technology — Biometric data interchange formats — Part 5: Face image data AMENDMENT 1: Conditions for taking photographs for face image data. Published 2007-12-15 5. Information technology — Biometric data interchange formats — Part 5: Face image data AMENDMENT 2: Three dimensional image data. 6. JTC 1/SC37/N3303. FCD text of the second edition. Contact pgrother AT nist DOT gov for more information.
PERFSTD INTEROP	ISO/IEC 19795-4 — Biometric Performance Testing and Reporting — Part 4: Interoperability Performance Testing. Posted as document 37N2370. The standard was published in 2007. It can be purchased from ANSI at http://webstore.ansi.org/.

www.ingramcontent.com/pod-product-compliance
Lightning Source LLC
Chambersburg PA
CBHW080442290526
45791CB00008BA/2582